D1133200

$mart Money
$hortcuts

$mart Money
$hortcuts
to Becoming Rich

by Tyler G. Hicks

Parker Publishing Company, Inc.

West Nyack, N. Y.

LIBRARY OF CONGRESS
CATALOG CARD NUMBER: 66-23356

Fifth printing . . . . March, 1968

PRINTED IN THE UNITED STATES OF AMERICA

81441 — B & P

YOU CAN HAVE EVERYTHING!

You *can* get rich—sooner than you think! The book you are now holding in your hands gives you hundreds of vital, powerful, and potent steps to becoming wealthy.

Here's what this book may do for you, if you put its recommendations to work and push your dreams to reality:

1. *You can become independently wealthy*, so you're no longer a slave to monthly payments on your car, the finance company, your home mortgage, or the local repairman.

2. *Get into a lucrative business of your own.* Forget taking orders from a surly boss and leap off the 9-to-5 treadmill. The shortcuts you're about to learn will jet you to new enthusiasm for building wealth in your own business, if this is what you want.

3. *Give your family the biggest income ever;* enjoy it together as your wealth grows. Buy the things your family needs and wants—the things your wife, or husband, has always dreamed of having.

4. *Live a glorious, productive, and happy life*—full of energy and good times. Travel all over the world; own a big car, or sporty racer; wear the best clothes; buy, and live in, your dream home; enjoy your hobby to the fullest, be it golf, fishing, hunting, boating, etc.; obtain the best medical attention; enjoy a safe, secure retirement, free of money worries.

5. *Obtain a top executive job, if you want one.* Know the prestige of a big office—and a matching salary. Enjoy a liberal expense account while you travel. Build your wealth through stock options, employment contracts, and other executive allowances.

You *can* become rich, if you really want to. Every year poor men become millionaires, proving that the often heard "You can't make a million dollars these days, taxes being what they are," is false. More people became millionaires in the last twenty years

7

—when tax rates were amongst the highest ever—than in the preceeding two hundred years. Your chances for success are greater than ever before.

Today's smart-money wealth builders use hundreds of profitable secret shortcuts to reduce the time and energy needed to earn a top-level income. You can use the same secret shortcuts, or you can invent new ones for yourself, as you read this book. Many of the magic secrets you'll acquire have never before been collected in one book.

The greatest feature of these magic smart-money secrets is that anyone can use them. Be you 9 or 90, man or woman, banker or baker, sailor or surveyor, they will work for you—again and again. You needn't be a college graduate to use these secret shortcuts, or even a high-school graduate. And as for starting capital, other than for a few dollars for paper and stamps, forget it. Your new money-making powers may rocket you to the sweetest problem known to man—what to do with all those dollars flooding into your bank.

Lastly, you will see the magic secret that tops all others— how, as a smart-money fortune builder, you can use OPM—other people's money—to build riches for yourself.

Let's begin now to make *you* rich. We'll take that thrilling, rewarding journey from just scraping by to a position in life where you have the riches that give you everything you want, and need, plus dollars and dollars to spare. You'll see how hundreds of others have built riches from a modest start. Your search and fulfillment will be easier because you have the specific directions in this book to zoom you on your way.

The next two hundred pages are packed with the shortcuts and techniques you need for your high-speed smart-money path to riches. Use them and watch your pot of gold grow and grow.
Good luck!

Tyler G. Hicks

CONTENTS

$mart Money

$hortcuts

CHAPTER 1

You Can Get Rich Quickly

You can get rich quickly—
if you really want wealth...

It isn't necessary to spend thirty years or more acquiring riches—if you know and use the magic smart money secret shortcuts to wealth described in this and the following chapters of this book. You can, if you apply yourself, become rich within three to five years after you begin the program given here.

With luck, you might earn a fortune in only three or four months. Then, if you wish, you can continue building greater wealth, or you can sit back and relax, enjoying your money. Take your choice—with money in your pocket you can afford to do so. Lord Rootes, who rose from a penny-an-hour laborer to multi-millionaire owner of Rootes Motors, said, "Money—i.e. wealth—gives you the freedom to spend your time doing what you enjoy most—be it work, play, or just plain dreaming." Even as long ago as 200 B.C., Plato recognized the value of riches when he remarked, "Wealth is a great comfort to any man."

Smart Money Wealth Builders Win

Some people earn money quickly in good times and bad, when the stock market is high or low, when the international situation is tense or calm. These people are often called *smart money wealth builders* because they keep the money flowing in no matter what happens. They earn a 33 to 100 per cent, or higher, profit on their money while less creative people earn only 5 per cent or lose money.

Twelve Smart Money Wealth Secrets

What are the secrets smart money wealth builders use to build riches fast? Here, for the first time anywhere, are their twelve basic secrets. Use these secrets on *your* magic shortcut path to wealth. When you use these powerful secrets you blast off to un-limited profits because as a smart money wealth builder:

- You go where the money is—and make it yours
- You seek riches every hour of the day
- You clearly see and understand your profit goals
- You gladly switch investments if necessary
- You accept, and take, business risks
- You actionize your search for riches
- You are ready to start small and grow big
- You jump into billion-dollar markets if possible
- You use other people's money to help build your own wealth
- You mine the secret wealth of your skills
- You diversify to millionize your income
- You find and market the unique, the unusual

Why the Twelve Secrets Work

Each of these twelve basic secrets, and many other little-known magic shortcuts, will become part of your subconscious skills as you read this book. You will quickly master the techniques for becoming rich in any business or profession you choose. These magic million-dollar methods will revolutionize your life, giving you an unlimited income. You will live the life you've always wanted. And, if you want, you can have a beautiful home, a powerful car, trips abroad, blue-chip securities, vacations galore, and anything else money can buy. Let's see how smart-money people use these secrets. Then you can do the same.

Smart Money People Seek Riches Every Hour

The smart money wealth builder likes money and pursues it relentlessly. While others may question this attitude, it's the smart money man or woman who builds riches quickly. Ernest T. Weir, founder of National Steel Corporation, sought riches because they would make him independent of the whims of others. Starting as a clerk, he became a millionaire. He worked long hours all his life—even after he became wealthy because he loved his business and enjoyed the profits he earned from it.

Can you become a smart money wealth builder? Yes, you can, if you're willing to recognize what money can do for you and are willing to seek it every hour of the day. You must be dedicated and persistent in your pursuit of riches. A relaxed, carefree approach to building riches seldom pays off. You can relax *after* you acquire your riches.

You are now ready to take the first step in your shortcut to riches. It is this:

> **Look for money-making opportunities every minute of every day. Begin the moment you wake up; continue looking until you go to sleep at night.**

Seek riches wherever you are—at work, during your lunch hour, while you travel, while you're at home, at local meetings of your club, religious group, school board, political party, or armed-forces reserve unit. Look for riches constantly and you'll uncover hundreds of ideas. You'll have so many ideas you'll soon be sharing them with your friends—for a slice of the profits. This will further increase your income.

Smart Money People Build Riches Fast

Paul J. Meyer, president of Success Motivation Institute, Inc., earned a million dollars in the insurance business by the time he was twenty-seven. Turning his back on an insurance income of more than $100,000 per year, he founded his Institute. Within three years it was a booming world-wide business.

Harry H., a real-estate investor, earned enough by the time he was twenty-two "not to have to worry any more." But he went on building his fortune until he and his partner joined the ranks of the largest real estate owners in Brooklyn and Manhattan. One of his biggest ventures in real estate came some twenty years after he became independently wealthy. That was the day he and his partners bought one of the largest buildings in the world.

At the other end of the age scale, Henry Reichman, made his first million dollars in about a year's time, *after* the age of fifty-five. His games for supermarkets—"Spell Cash" and "Split the Dollar"—brought him ten million dollars in a recent year. Reichman thinks that the greatest feature of his success is that he hit the big money after the age of fifty-five, when he was "a man who couldn't get the attention of an office boy if I were looking for a job in a corporation."

My good friend, Sam Miller, founded his famous advertising agency as a one-man shop at the age of fifty-five. Within a few years he had a staff of 70 people and a booming business.

Colonel Harland Sanders, a 65-year-old retiree, used the proceeds of his first social security check to finance his travels to franchise his Kentucky Fried Chicken recipe. He drove his car to hundreds of cities, selling more than one thousand franchises throughout the United States. English, Canadian, and Japanese businessmen also bought his franchise. If his funds ran low on his travels, he drove back to Kentucky and waited for his monthly social-security check. Then he was off again on his journeys. Within ten years, sales of Kentucky Fried Chicken were more than one-hundred million dollars a year.

So you see, you can use these magic secret shortcuts at any age, in any place, in any business, to build your riches.

Thousands of intelligent, capable, smart money people earn their fortunes quickly, every year. The fortune hunter anxious to find and use the magic and secret shortcuts to riches is in such a hurry that he can't afford to lose money when a market he's in (stock, real estate, commodity, etc.) is declining. So he usually manages to show a good profit while his friends are crying about their losses. You can earn while others lose if you apply the secrets given in this book.

Smart Money People Aren't Sentimental

You can't be sentimental about your investments and make money from them. Thus, if you invest in a piece of property because you love the color of its trees in autumn, you are buying for senti-mental reasons, not economic reasons. True, you may find someone else who loves autumn scenes more than you do and who may be willing to pay you twice what you paid for the property. Autumn, however, comes but once a year and is often short. Thus, your profit potential is restricted.

The smart money man buys property because he believes he sees a profit potential in it. His future profits may come from a good location, attractive view, or natural mineral deposits. He analyzes the property from a profit standpoint, not from the per-sonal aspect of what he likes to see in a lawn or some other tempo-rary feature. This is your second magic shortcut to riches:

> **Seek permanent, long-term profit potential in every deal you enter. Buy for profit potential, not for personal non-business appeal.**

Be careful to distinguish between your business and non-business likes and dislikes. So long as business considerations govern your thinking you're relatively safe. The only risks you run are business risks. When you introduce personal, non-business likes and dislikes into your business thinking, your risks multiply by the thousands and your profit chances sink dangerously low.

Smart Money People Switch Investments

The smart money man never "falls in love" with his investments unless they are showing superior profits. He's always ready and willing to sell out a low-profit investment and buy into a new or different one promising higher profits. Being light on your financial feet can bring you big profits fast.

Bob K., a steamship executive, learned several years ago the value of being willing to switch investments. He was interested in art and bought several paintings for a new cooperative apartment he and his wife planned to buy. Bob put a $100 deposit on the apartment and waited for construction to be completed.

As work progressed on the apartment house, Bob noted that the remaining apartments were quickly sold. He mentioned this to the building agent, who replied, "Sure we're sold out. But we still have hundreds of buyers looking for apartments. You could sell yours right now for a $3,000 profit if you wanted to." Bob went home and thought it over. He checked into other desirable co-ops and found that in almost every case the tenant could sell at a profit before moving in.

Not satisfied to stop at co-ops, Bob checked new private homes in his area. To his amazement and delight, he found that he could do the same—put a deposit on a house and sell before moving in.

Talking the prospects over with his wife, Bob decided to sell his co-op and not move. He sold—at a $3,200 profit—after only four months.

He also decided to speculate in other co-ops and private homes. So he sold the paintings at a modest profit and immediately invested the entire income from the paintings and the apartment in a number of co-op apartments and in several private homes. Today Bob is a wealthy man. But he's ready to switch out of co-ops and homes into something more lucrative as soon as the market drops.

To date he has always made a profit on his buying, holding, and selling plan.

The smart money man may be in diamonds this year, real estate next year, and Liberty ships the third year. Franz Pick, famous owner of Pick Publications and a world-wide authority on money problems, points out that, during a recent year, mercury was "fantastic". A flask of mercury, purchased at $235 on January 2, was worth $485 one year later—a rise of $250 per flask. This is more than a 100 per cent profit. A flask of mercury is a convenient item to store—compared with a Liberty ship, which rose 80 per cent in value during the same year.

Other items making big profits for smart-money men in recent years are antimony, copper, platinum, lead, and zinc. Tapestries, snuffboxes, paintings, and sculptured objects are also money makers. Thus, you can be cultured or unassuming, a businessman, teacher, lawyer, doctor, or production-line worker, and still be a smart-money builder. Formal education is *not* a requirement for learning the shortcuts to becoming rich by switching from unprofitable to profitable investments. This provides our third magic shortcut step to riches:

> **Seek and find profitable investments. Switch out of unprofitable investments into profitable ones. Never hold an unprofitable investment for sentimental reasons.**

Risks and Riches Go Together

"There's no safe way to get rich," says my good friend, John K., who made several million dollars in the construction business. "The man who gets rich fast often takes more risks than the man who spends thirty or forty years building his wealth. Gamble big—win big; gamble small—win small."

Risk-taking frightens most of us. We have enough problems in life without adding business risks. True—but if you seek a safe, fully insured road to riches, you'll never find it. The shortcut road to riches is strewn with risks—large and small. Learn to face these risks; live with them without fear, and you sky-rocket your chances for success in your search for riches.

Banish fear by facing your risks now. Your biggest business risks are:

RISK	CURE
1. Business failure	Work to pay off bills; switch to a profitable business
2. Reduced income	Devise ways to increase the income—advertise; hold contests; give prizes
3. Excessive competition	Offer something the competition cannot—lower prices, bigger servings, personalized service

Challenge fear and you defeat it. Run away from fear and you will suffer in its grips until you lose the fight. Risk-taking almost becomes enjoyable when you earn a profit from it. Try a few business risks and see for yourself.

Get Ready for Action in Your Wealth Search

Your subconscious is now conditioned for the million-dollar shortcut path to wealth. You will daily

- Look for money-making opportunities everywhere
- Seek permanent, long-term profitable deals
- Switch out of unprofitable deals into profitable ones
- Be willing to take necessary business risks

With this four-step approach you are certain to increase your income. Your riches will grow, day by day, hour by hour. You will soon have more money than you ever thought possible. From now on, every trend in your financial future should be positive, profitable, powerful, and promising. Now let's take action on your search for riches.

CHAPTER 2

Choose A Smart Money Path to Your Fortune

*There are thousands of ways
for you to become rich ...*

Some ways will bring you money faster than others; some require less time and energy than others. What we want to do, here and now, is to help you pick a smart money path to riches that will make you wealthy as quickly as possible. Perhaps you may even reach the level of H. L. Hunt, said to be one of the world's wealthiest men, and worth some seven billion dollars. His income is more than one million dollars per day! Yet H. L. Hunt began with little capital but much ambition and drive.

Decide What You Do Best

Each of us has skills and talents different from the next person. Your skills and talents are unique; your knowledge of certain aspects of business may be the key to your fortune. Or a combination of your existing skills and talents with new ones, or those of another person, may bring you the riches you seek.

Get out a pencil and fill in the *Riches Skills Checklist* below. Answer each question as accurately as possible. Take your time; don't rush. The answers you give will aid you in choosing the shortest and most profitable path to wealth.

RICHES SKILLS CHECKLIST

1. To date my largest income has come from ....
2. My favorite way of earning money is ....
3. People often tell me I do .... well.
4. I .... (do; do not) enjoy working with the general public.
5. Figuring profits and losses .... (does; does not) interest me.
6. Risking money .... (does; does not) frighten me.
7. My father .... (did; did not) have his own business.
8. I .... (do; do not) get along well with most people.
9. Working for someone else .... (does; does not) interest me.
10. I .... (have; have not) a strong desire for money.

Study your answers; they will reveal much about your wealth-building skills. If your answers to (1) and (2) are the same, you won't have to search for a new way to wealth. If (3) agrees with the first two, you can concentrate on those activities that brought you the best return in the past.

If your answers to (1), (2), and (3) are different, study your replies to (4) through (10). If (4), (5), and (6) are yes-type answers—i.e. you do enjoy working with people, figuring profits, and risking money, consider going into business for yourself as the path for your fortune. But before rushing into a business, study (7) through (10).

If your father was in his own business (7), you get along with most people (8), and working for someone else *does not* interest you (9), you are probably ideally suited for a business of your own. Lastly, you must have a strong desire for money (10). If you don't, your chances for building wealth quickly are very small.

You May Have Top-Executive Skills

What if your answers (2), (3), (4), (5), (6), (7), and (9) show that your greatest interest lie in working for someone else—say in a large or small corporation? Is all your hope for attaining riches lost? Certainly not!

Nathan Cummings, a skillful businessman, went broke in the shoe manufacturing business. Within a few years he built a booming bakery business. He retired at the age of 42 but soon found that he enjoyed working more than relaxing. He heard of a good business for sale but he couldn't buy it because his funds were tied up elsewhere. So he went to work for the company he wanted to buy and in less than two years he raised the company's earnings to a level where he obtained enough credit to buy the company without investing any of his own cash. Today Nathan Cummings is chairman of the company—Consolidated Foods Corporation— the largest independent food wholesaler in the United States. He combines the ability to work *for* others with the ability to work *with* others. You can do the same, if you analyze your skills and concentrate on them in your search for riches.

Learn How Money Is Earned Quickly

People get rich quickly most often by applying one of six different principles:

1. **By selling a low-cost product to a large market**
   (*For example:* Hula hoops; skate boards; plastic raincaps for women; 007 (James Bond) labelled products)
2. **By selling a high-cost product to a limited few**
   (*For example:* Rare paintings; unusual gems; handcrafted ship models)

3. **By buying a sluggish product or organization and giving it new life**
   (*For example:* A declining manufacturing firm; an outmoded rest home; a neglected nightclub)
4. **By going where the money is and earning some of it**
   (*For example:* Selling fuel oil in a new housing development; placing refrigerated vending machines in areas with few stores; selling to teenagers in suburban areas)
5. **By using skill or knowledge to become an insider**
   (*For example:* Developing or inventing a new product or process and selling or licensing it; merging two firms having common interests; buying into a growing situation)
6. **By using borrowed capital to build an income**
   (*For example:* Buying real estate with borrowed money; buying a going business; buying low-cost items for resale)

These six paths to financial peace of mind give magical results. You'll learn more about their startling power in later chapters. For now, all you need to do is think about the possibilities for you in each of these six paths to wealth.

You Can Get Rich In Some Jobs

Are the six big opportunities listed above the only ways to become rich today? Certainly not! There are thousands of other ways. For instance, you could become president of a large automotive concern and earn $180,000 per year in salary with an additional cash bonus of $560,000 per year, along with stock options equal to one-third of the cash bonus. Or you might set your sights a little lower and aim at a $140,000-per-year salary and a $100,000-per-year annual cash bonus in aircraft and missile manufacturing.

There's just one item you must remember about these and similar jobs—top-level spots in large corporations are difficult to obtain, are few in number, and usually require many years of apprenticeship before you are appointed. As one president of a large corporation remarked, "Sure, I earn big money. But the trouble is I'm almost too old to enjoy it. Besides, I put in so many years working up to this spot that I can't think of anything but the company—it's my whole life."

There are only about five hundred top executive jobs paying over $100,000 per year in the United States. In other countries there are far fewer such jobs. Add to this the heavy tax burden when all your income is in salary and bonuses, and the idea of becoming rich through a job becomes less and less appealing. Remember, though, that some people do it every year. You may be one of them!

Just keep in mind the problems you face: few jobs and thousands of candidates; long apprenticeship; extreme competition and tension on the job. If you still want to take this route to riches, go ahead. You'll learn many techniques the pros use when you read later chapters in this book.

Seven Who Hit the Big Money

Frank G. Jameson invested $3,000 to start an electronics company when he was 31. To raise this money he borrowed on the little property he owned. Just four years passed before Frank sold his stock in the company for $1.8 million. Today he controls 14 different businesses. How did Frank build his first fortune? By using borrowed capital to build an income (Principle 6).

Else Frankfurt, partner in Page Boy Maternity Co., Inc., started her dress business with a capital of only $250. In 15 years she was a millionairess. How did she build her wealth? By selling a low-cost product to a large market. (Principle 1). Her product: maternity skirts with a hole in them which allows adjustment of the drape.

William P. Lear started an electrical shop at the ripe age of 13. Ten years later he was earning $2,000 per month as a radio specialist. He obtained more than 100 patents. Soon he founded Lear, Inc., later Lear Siegler, Inc., which did $90 million per year in electronics and avionics business. Today he heads Lear Jet Corp., builders of one of the fastest small jets in the world. How does Bill Lear earn his money? By selling a high-cost product to a limited few (Principle 2). His jet sells for $500,000 up. He figures he's so wealthy he "could spend $1,000 a day until he was 100" (about 40 years)—"and I'd just begin to nibble into the principal."

William Begel started his business career as a chemical engineer knowing several languages including Russian. During his spare time he began translating foreign technical books into English. Soon he and a partner started a translation business with hardly any capital. Within six years his firm, Scripta Technica, reached the million-dollar mark, and is still growing rapidly.

Charles Lecht ran a computer installation in the Army. When he was discharged he went to work for a computer company. Soon he decided to go into business for himself as a "softwear" specialist—debugging computers and preparing special programs. Starting with almost no capital and little business experience, his firm, Advanced Computer Techniques Corporation, grew from one man to 51 people in three years. Business during the third year approached nearly one million dollars and the firm continued to boom.

How do Bill Begel and Charlie Lecht earn their money? By using skill or knowledge to become an insider (Principle 5). You can do the same if you have unique skills or knowledge. There are thousands of firms and individuals seeking people with unique skills or knowledge. Cash in on this need and you, too, can become wealthy.

Angelo Caputo took over a small fuel-oil business after working as a fuel truck driver for $40 a week. Sensing a boom in home building thirty miles from his small headquarters, Caputo opened a branch office in the new area. When the homes went up, so did the demand for his oil. Fifteen years later his firm was doing $7 million a year in business. Today Caputo has many other interests—real estate, bowling alleys, an industrial park, a motel, office buildings, a heating and plumbing company, and an oil tanker handling more than 80 million gallons of oil per year. How did Angelo Caputo become a millionaire? By going where the money was and earning some of it. (Principle 4). You can do the same, if you study where the money is and go out and earn some of it.

James Bruyn, an ex-insurance man, had a friend in the fishing-tackle business. This friend ran his business in a rented loft.

During a regular inspection of the loft the man found more than 1,000 small (about 4 x 5-in.) hand looms in a dark corner. Questioning the building owner, the fishing-tackle man learned that the owner had invented the loom and wanted to sell the patent. The fishing-tackle man bought the loom and began a small mail-order business to sell it. He sold most of the looms when James Bruyn came across one at the fishing-tackle man's home. Bruyn saw big possibilities for the loom and bought the patent from his friend. Soon James Bruyn was receiving 20 orders a day for the loom that retails for $1.98. Then an article on the loom ran in *Woman's Day* magazine and the orders zoomed to about 2,000 per day. His local post office sends a mail truck to his shop twice a day to deliver the orders. To make the loom more useful, Mrs. Bruyn prepared a book of designs for the loom. The book retails for 25 cents. How did James Bruyn move into big sales? By buying a sluggish product and giving it new life (Principle 3). There are many products and organizations that you can rejuvenate with new ideas. Later you'll learn how and where to find products and organizations you can convert from losers to profitable winners.

Your Chances are Better in Your Own Business

The seven live-wire people described above are just a few of the thousands of men and women who earn big money in their own businesses every year. While you can become rich in a job— if you're lucky—chances for big earnings are much greater in a business of your own.

I know hundreds of executives—men and women earning from $20,000 to $100,000, and more, per year. They are capable, talented people. Yet almost every one of them will tell you, in a moment of confidence, that they *know* they could earn more in a business of their own, or by combining a business of their own with work for a large company.

If you feel that an income of $20,000 to $100,000 per year is enough to make you rich, this book will show you how to combine the exhilarating freedom of your own business with the security offered by a large corporation. For no matter how you approach the problem of becoming rich in a hurry, your chances are much better in a business of your own, or with a combination of your own business with an executive job.

Choose Your Smart Money Path Now

You can dream of riches for years but your dreams won't put money in your pocket unless you take action. "Action separates the men from the boys—the rich from the 9-to-5 slaves," says a good friend of mine who became independently wealthy in three years in the construction business.

We all know people who are constantly on the verge of a *big killing* but never seem to earn big money. Why is this? The reason these people never hit the big money is because they spend most of their time and energy talking about what they plan to do. But they have so little time and energy left after all their talk that they never put their dreams into action.

Last year I financed a younger brother of mine in a business venture. The negotiations were prolonged and involved. While the negotiations were in progress my brother and I told a number of people about the business, its current income, and its future prospects. We were both amazed at the reactions of these people. *Every person told us we were making a mistake.* Some said it was the wrong business; others said it was the wrong time to go into business; still others said it was wrong to do business with relatives. Today my brother's business is booming and promises to grow every year. Yet every person who felt like giving us free advice is in exactly the same spot as a year ago. These people are waiting for the ideal business at a bargain price in the most convenient location. You can wait forever for this kind of business and it will never come to you.

Why did my brother succeed? Because he took action on his dreams of a business of his own. He (1) decided what kind of a business he wanted, (2) began an active search for this business by studying ads, visiting nearby businesses of the same kind, (3) collected information on income, costs, problems, and profits, (4) carefully studied the traffic flow in each business he considered buying, (5) compared statements made by the seller with the information collected earlier, (6) bought the business he thought was the best for him after determining that it measured up to his requirements.

You can take these six steps and win. John Bloom, who rose from a $34-a-week clerk to a multimillionaire heading a $40-million business in four years, took similar steps. He analyzed the market for washing machines in England and decided that he could sell more machines by going directly to the customer, instead of using the normal retail outlets. He was right in his analysis and within less than five years he had a personal fortune said to approach $2.8 million.

Samuel Cooke took a similar tack when, at age 11, he began selling vegetables directly to housewives, door to door. He rose to board chairman of Penn Fruit Company, directing 50 supermarkets in four states. Sam Cooke invented the checkout counter while working with Clarence Saunders, who founded the Piggley Wiggley chain of supermarkets. In building his door-to-door vegetable business to 50 supermarkets, Sam Cooke employed the six success principles previously listed.

For years you can dream, plan, hope, and imagine how much money you'll make when you stumble on the right business or job. But you'll never find the right business or job until you take action—that is, go out and find the business or job that will make you rich. You can begin that action here and now by completing the *Wealth Action Chart* below. Do it now—and put yourself on the road to wealth.

WEALTH ACTION CHART

1. The way I'd like to become rich is by ....
   (speculating in real estate; becoming president of my company, etc.).
2. I've heard of .... (few; many) people becoming wealthy this way.
3. Today, ... (month, day, year) I plan to begin an active search for a business or job of this type by ....
   (studying ads, visiting business brokers, applying at employment agencies, etc.).
4. I will collect complete information on this business beginning ....
   .... (date) and will complete my search by ....
   (date). I will obtain this information from ....
   (libraries, government agencies, businessmen, etc.).
5. I expect to find a suitable business or job by ....

(date). If I have not found a business or job by the above date I will continue looking for .... weeks.
6. Once a suitable business or job is located I will study it thoroughly for .... weeks. During this study I will carefully compare actual operating facts and data with facts and data uncovered during my research.
7. I will buy the business or take the job within .... days after my study is finished.

Adapt Quick Riches to Your Skills

Suppose you tried to fill out the *Wealth Action Chart* above and found you were stumped by Action 1. What should you do? Give up? Forget quick riches? No! Never give up! If you have the drive and desire for fast wealth, continue your search. Read on, because you are about to discover how you can adapt quick riches to *your* skills.

Take some time today to analyze your true wealth-building skills *now*. Study the following skills list and check your strength for each skill. Be objective—this is a secret test for yourself. Start now.

SKILLS STRENGTH ANALYSIS

SKILL	MY STRENGTH RATING			
	High	Good	Fair	None
1. Business arithmetic	——	——	——	——
2. Salesmanship	——	——	——	——
3. Getting along with people	——	——	——	——
4. Outdoor sports	——	——	——	——
5. Intellectual activities	——	——	——	——
6. Manual work	——	——	——	——
7. Management	——	——	——	——

Study this analysis of your skills. Where do you rate *good* or *high*? These are the skills that are most likely to earn big money for you. Once you know your best skills, find a suitable business or job for building your riches by using the *Action Analysis Chart* below.

ACTION ANALYSIS CHART

SKILL	BUSINESS OF YOUR OWN IN WHICH YOU CAN USE THIS SKILL	JOB IN WHICH YOU CAN USE THIS SKILL
1. Business arithmetic	Stock market; rental real estate; business finance; land speculation; commodity markets; etc.	Securities analyst; comptroller; corporate finance; stock broker; product manager; etc.
2. Salesmanship	Sales agency for national product; franchised product sales; freelance selling of a line of your own or others' products; etc.	Salesman for expensive product line; sales manager; vice-president of sales; training of salesmen; etc.
3. Getting along with people	Restaurant; dance studio; billiard room; tavern; manufacturer's representative; agent for actors, writers or artists; employment agency; etc.	Public relations director; sales agent; recruiter; personnel manager; etc.
4. Outdoor sports	Sports instruction; sporting-goods store; sports tours; guide service; rental of sporting equipment; etc.	Employed instructor; manager of sport store or department; sports adviser; etc.
5. Intellectual activities	Private tutor; financial adviser; art-gallery owner; bookstore owner; advertising agency owner; etc.	Advertising chief copywriter; magazine or book editor; newspaper editor or publisher; etc.
6. Manual work	Gas-station; marina; plumbing; aircraft rental and repair; heating and air conditioning; etc.	Chief mechanic; chief engineer; head toolmaker; etc.
7. Management	Management consulting; executive recruiting; publish business advice; etc.	Organization president or executive; government adviser; etc.

Take Positive Action Today

Enter here three smart money paths to wealth,

1. ....
2. ....
3. ....

you'd like to follow, based on your findings in this chapter, and your personal preferences. Take positive action on these paths today by continuing to read this book. As you read you'll prepare yourself for a greater income in your chosen activity. You'll also learn many dollar-laden techniques that can help you earn more money faster. Remember: YOU CAN BUILD WEALTH QUICKLY IF YOU CHOOSE A SMART MONEY PATH TO YOUR FORTUNE.

CHAPTER 3

Actionize Your Search For Wealth

To earn a large income quickly...

... you must know what you're doing, no matter how humble this work may be. Orville Caesar, who became president of the largest bus company in the world, the famous Greyhound Line, started his business career as a garage mechanic working for an automobile agency. He rose to chief of the repair department and saved his money. Soon he had enough to buy the auto agency.

As part of his purchase, Mr. Caesar received two truck

chassis. Loving to tinker, Mr. Caesar designed and built bus bodies
on the chassis because there was no other market for the chassis.
Noting that people wanted to travel quickly between Superior,
Wisconsin and Duluth, Minnesota, Mr. Caesar opened a bus line
using two salvaged chassis. Soon he had so little time for selling cars
that he sold the auto agency so he could concentrate on his expanding transit business. Later he merged his company with the Greyhound Line, which began with even more meager capital. The
merged companies grew to a business owning more than 5,000
buses.

Both Orville Caesar and Carl Wickman, with whom he
merged, knew the transportation business. When there was some
aspect of the business they didn't fully understand, or were unable
to obtain full data on, they immediately studied it. This knowledge
enabled them to stay ahead of competition and build the world's
largest bus line. You, too, need knowledge if you want to build
wealth rapidly, no matter what type of business or job you choose.
Let's see how you can do it.

Begin with a Shelf of Good Books

When you first begin your search for quick riches you will
probably have few friends who know or understand your goals. If
you're married, your wife or husband may not be too interested in
the *methods* you use although they certainly will be most interested
in the *results*. This is a common situation—don't worry about it.
You can easily acquire what some men believe are the best friends
in the world—good business books.

In Chapter 2 you chose the business or job you believe
offers the best promise of quick wealth. No matter what this business or job is—from acorn growing to importing Zulu artifacts—
there is a book, article, catalog, pamphlet, or other printed docu-
ment discussing it. All you need do is locate it. You'll learn exactly
how in this chapter.

Divide your business library into two parts—(1) general
information on broad business or job procedures—billing, records,
taxes, etc., or company organization, personnel practices, financial
analysis, etc., depending on the method you chose to build wealth

quickly—a business or a job; (2) specific information on the business or job you chose. The second, or specific section of your library, will reflect your individual interests and will provide valuable dollar-generating ideas you can use for years. In my own quick wealth-building efforts, all of which have been outstandingly successful, several specialized books I purchased at prices of $5 to $10 each, have returned more than $5000 income *each*. This is a return of 100,000 per cent! Now do you question the financial value of a good business library? Remember this golden action key:

When first starting your search for wealth, good business books may be your best and only friends.

Develop Your General Library

Here are twelve excellent books I've found useful in building my general knowledge of business procedures. I'm sure that you'll also find them highly useful. But before rushing out to buy any of these books, visit your local library and examine each of the books. You'll find that most good libraries will have these books on their shelves. I suggest that you buy the low-priced paperbacks— 25¢ to $1.95—sight unseen since you can more than recover your investment from each book, even if you obtain only one useful idea from each. Almost all the listed books are what I call "baby classics"—that is, they have been around long enough to be in their second, or later, edition. Since these books will continue to be available for many years, I've omitted the publication date from each.

Study each of these books carefully and you may be able to duplicate Melisande Marano's feat. Starting from scratch, never having worked in business before, she built a million-dollar greeting-card business in three years. She calls her products "the costliest greeting cards in the world." Her first office was in the basement of her home; as the business grew, she had to move to a plant. Besides greeting cards, Melisande Marano sells imported art books—some at prices of $100 each. One book, a fascimile of an antique illuminated Bible, sells for $1,800 per copy!

You can teach yourself the facts you'll need in business to

help you build a profitable new income. Begin reading the following aids *now*:

CLOTHBOUND

John N. Myer, *Accounting for Non-Accountants,* American Research Council

J. K. Lasser, *Business Management Handbook,* McGraw-Hill Book Company

George N. Kahn, *The 36 Biggest Mistakes Salesmen Make and How to Correct Them,* Prentice-Hall, Inc.

Auren Uris, *Mastery of People,* Prentice-Hall, Inc.

A.E. McNelly and L.J. Adams, *Business Arithmetic,* Prentice-Hall, Inc.

A.L. Lavine, *Modern Business Law,* Prentice-Hall, Inc.

PAPERBACKS

S.G. Kling, *Handy Legal Adviser,* Permabooks

U.S. Dept. of Commerce, *Guides for Business Analysis and Profit Evaluation,* U.S. Government Printing Office

B. LaSalle Woelfel, *Guides for Profit Planning,* U.S. Government Printing Office

M.R. Greene, *Insurance and Risk Management for Small Business,* U.S. Government Printing Office

Jack Zwick, *A Handbook of Small Business Finance,* U.S. Government Printing Office

Wesley Johnson, *How to Increase Your Selling Power,* Northwest Nazarene College

Books That Build Job Skills

Suppose, however, that you'd prefer to build your fortune on a job because you agree with R. H. Cabell and say, "I like business because it is competitive, because it rewards deeds rather than words . . . it promptly penalizes inefficiency, while rewarding well those who give it the best they have in them." Here are twelve excellent books that will help you build your job skills.

CLOTHBOUND

Bernard Haldane, *How to Make a Habit of Success,* Prentice-Hall, Inc.

Auren Uris, *The Executive Job Market,* McGraw-Hill Book Company

William E. Edwards, *10 Days to a Great New Life,* Prentice-Hall, Inc.

Joseph G. Mason, *How to Be a More Creative Executive,* McGraw-Hill Book Company

Frederick Dyer, et al., *Putting Yourself Over in Business,* Prentice-Hall, Inc.

David J. Schwartz, *The Magic of Thinking Big,* Prentice-Hall, Inc.

PAPERBACKS

Ordway Tead, *The Art of Administration,* McGraw-Hill Book Company

Fred V. Gardner, *Profit Management and Control,* McGraw-Hill Book Company

Norman V. Peale, *The Power of Positive Thinking,* Fawcett Publications, Inc.

George Anderson, *How to Make Correct Decisions,* Macfadden-Bartell Corporation

Walter K. Gutman, *You Only Have to Get Rich Once,* Bantam Books, Inc.

Samuel G. Kling, *Handy Legal Adviser for Home and Business,* Permabooks.

Build Your Specialized Library

In Chapter 2 you chose your path to a smart money fortune—either a business of your own or a high-paying job. Now you are ready to take action on that choice. The best way to start is by building a specialized library specifically for *your* fortune-building needs. Here is a golden action key most people overlook:

Build a specialized library and you can uncover the smart-money secrets of the most successful people in the world. Your library can repay you thousands of times its cost.

Most people scoff at book learning as a way to a fortune. And most people remain relatively poor throughout their lives— living from one paycheck to the next. You don't scoff at book learning as a way to a fortune. You recognize, as does every smart money fortune builder, that you must learn your business if you are to succeed quickly. John Henry Patterson, who founded National Cash Register Company with an investment of $6,500, used charts, films, slides, conferences, conventions, and books to teach his employees important business facts. His firm grew from 13 employees and a capital of $6,500 to the world's largest manu-facturer of cash registers with more than $200-million in working capital.

Chapter 2 helped you choose your smart money path to wealth. Now pick the specialized books that will help you acquire that wealth. Go to your nearest public library and obtain these four books from the reference shelf: *Subject Guide to Books*; *Books in Print*; *Paperbound Books in Print*; and *How-To-Do-It Books*. Each is published by R. R. Bowker Company. The first two are issued annually; the second two are issued at less frequent intervals.

Look up your chosen activity in each of these books. You'll find useful books on almost every activity that interests you— from abacus to zoology. The books on your specialty will form the basis of your specialized library. Read as many of these books as you can. Some will appeal to you more strongly than others. Buy these books and make them the main titles in your specialized library.

Does hunting for and evaluating these books take you a long time? No! Your entire search is confined to four reference books and the dozen or two specialized titles that interest you. Here's another golden action key most people never use:

Study several books on one topic and quickly acquire valuable fortune-building knowledge. By using several books

**you acquire information from more than one expert. This
enables you to build skills based on broad experience. You
progress faster.**

In later chapters you'll find lists of many specialized books.
Use these if they are in your area of interest. If not, refer to the
four Bowker reference books listed above.

Use the Important Periodicals

I know many smart money fortune builders. We often
discuss their fortune-building techniques. Almost every fortune
builder reads extensively. And many of them read the same
periodicals—i.e. newspapers and magazines. Hundreds of these
wealthy men and women tell me they regularly read

NEWSPAPERS

The Wall Street Journal
The New York Times

MAGAZINES

Business Week
Fortune

These two newspapers and magazines form the core of your
periodicals reading.

From these, branch out to the specialized business magazines covering the field you've chosen in which to build your
wealth. There is at least one, and sometimes many more, magazine or magazines covering your special area unless that area is
completely new and untried in every way. Refer to copies of
*Standard Rate and Data—Business Publications, The Writer's
Market,* and *Gebbie House Magazine Directory* at your local
library. These three references list nearly 10,000 specialized publications. You're sure to find one or more suitable publications in
the lists.

Obtain free copies of the periodicals that interest you by

writing to the publisher requesting several recent issues. Read every business article *and* advertisement in each issue of the magazine. Soak up every fact, statistic, and sales estimate you can. Make yourself a walking authority on your chosen activity. If you don't understand some of the words you read, buy a good specialized dictionary (see the Bowker books), or send a list of the difficult words to the editor of one of the magazines. He'll be delighted to help you.

Read the two newspapers and two magazines listed above for at least a year. They are obtainable by mail subscriptions no matter where you live or your local library may have them. You'll learn quickly, thoroughly. You'll soon see the truth of this golden key to quick riches:

> **Build your over-all business skills by regularly reading the best periodicals. Learn the thoughts of the wealthiest men in business today. Use periodicals whether you seek wealth through a job or business.**

Get a Place to Work

Up to now you've been gathering facts—you're like the runner who has trained himself for the race. Once his body is in condition he needs a track on which to run. Once your mind is prepared, you're ready to start serious work towards your wealth goal.

Select a room, or a corner of a room, in your home where you'll do your work. Tell your wife or husband that you plan to work in that room or corner and you don't want anything disturbed. You may get some objections—tell her or him that it is extremely important to both of you that you have a place to work. John Diebold, founder of a large consulting firm in the automation field, began working in the corner of a bedroom in his family home. Today his firm has world-wide offices noted for their beautiful decorations and profitable operation.

Obtain a one- or two-drawer file. If you can't afford a file, go to a supermarket and get two or three cardboard boxes 12-in. wide and 8-in. high. Incline them at a slight angle so your papers lean against the back and you have an excellent temporary file.

Next, obtain an 8½ x 11-in. looseleaf binder and a supply of ruled and plain paper. The looseleaf binder, your files, and your "office" now make it official—you are ready to start building your fortune quickly. You are ready to put another golden action key to work:

> **Commit yourself to building a quick fortune by getting a place to work and the needed equipment—files and records. Taking this first step will put you on the road to wealth.**

Take Action—Observe and Record

Chapter 2 guided your choice of your smart money path to wealth. It could be any of the thousands of ways people have built wealth. Now that you've made a choice and have facilities to work, observe and record what you read, see, hear, and learn. Use your files and looseleaf notebook for your records.

Billy Rose, the great showman, investor, and art collector, decided early in life that he wanted to write hit songs so he could build his wealth and skills. Having made his choice (Chapter 2), he actionized his search for wealth (Chapter 3) by getting a place to work, observe, and record. Billy's place to work was the New York Public Library where he studied the lyrics and melodies of popular hit tunes for the previous one hundred years. From these he developed what he considered the best theory for writing songs. Using his observations and information, Billy went on to write more than twenty hit songs, including "It's Only a Paper Moon" and "I Want to Be Loved". He rapidly increased his income because he applied many of the unusual techniques used by intelligent and capable wealth builders. You are now learning these techniques. If you wish, you can use them in your chosen field.

As a young man, H. L. Meckler began work in the transportation field as a freight cashier because he believed "the transportation field had important capabilities". Called "Meck" by his friends, the young man observed and studied the transportation business. Eventually he became president of a truck-leasing company. He was liked by his company and he enjoyed his job. But he wanted a business of his own (Chapter 2). Starting with only

$1,000, Meck built Lease Plan International to a $100-million per year business. Today his truck and car leasing business continues to grow faster than ever.

Observe—look about you. Note how well, or how poorly, other people are doing in your chosen business or job. Make notes; record them in your looseleaf book. Divide the book into suitable sections—Income; Profits; Problems; Personnel; Location; etc.

Prepare a special section for Ideas. Enter every idea you get in this section. The more you think about your business or job, the greater the number of ideas you'll get. Some of these ideas may be top-notch, worth many dollars to you. Write them down as soon as they come to you—if you don't, you may forget.

Read—learn what is going on in your field. Make notes of what you learn. Build a reservoir of new, useful, valuable information. When you read the specialized periodicals, note which firms supply free catalogs. Write for them; study the catalogs when they arrive.

Steve K. had a severe fright on his executive job recently. Something happened on his job that made him think he might be fired. Steve had never thought about being fired before and he was shaken. That evening he sat down and analyzed what he would do if he were fired. He found that he could live three or four months on his savings—then he'd be short of cash. So for the next several weeks Steve studied newspaper Help Wanted and Employment Agency ads. One agency ad featured the expression *Job Continuation Insurance*. Steve's mind jumped to a variation of this—*Salary Continuation Insurance*. This would be a plan, Steve mused, whereby any executive or other worker could, by paying a small weekly fee, buy insurance to guarantee the continuation of his salary for one year, two years, or longer, after he was fired or laid off from his job.

Today Steve is working out his Salary Continuation Insurance. This insurance will supplement state employment insurance, guaranteeing a person an income equal to his or her present salary for at least one year. Steve expects that the low cost of the insurance—about $1 per week per $100 per week take-home pay, will attract many workers to his plan. Thus, one good idea, gleaned by observation and reading, is about to pay off. Steve wasn't fired but hopes to be able to quit as soon as he markets his insurance.

Talk to people in the business or on the job you chose to build your quick fortune. Listen to what these people say about the business or job, its problems, advantages, drawbacks. Make notes of everything important you hear. Be alert for new, untried ideas. Everyone in business and on a job has dreams of what he would, or could, do, "If I only had the time and the money." You might be able to take one of these ideas and turn it into profit for yourself. The world is full of people who sit and dream but do nothing to actionize their dreams. This leads to our next golden action key:

> **Seek information, facts, ideas, methods, and skills you'll need to build a quick fortune. Enter into your notebook everything valuable you learn. Watch your confidence and skills grow as your knowledge increases.**

Establish An Action Base

If you've read this book attentively this far, you've probably sensed that I'm somewhat partial to building a fortune through a business of your own. There are many reasons for this—but the main reason is that more people build big fortunes in a business of their own than through holding a job. Mads Clausen, a Dane, founded Danfoss, one of Denmark's largest companies, in the attic of his father's farmhouse. Today his annual sales exceed $70 million and Clausen owns the entire company.

Suppose, however, that you want to build your fortune through a job. What good is an action base? Plenty, as you'll see shortly.

Try This Simple Action Base for Wealth

The best action base for building a quick fortune is a business of your own. You can establish a business for $50 or less, depending on where you live. All you need is a

1. Company name
2. Business address

3. Telephone number
4. Letterhead
5. Files and record book

Let's take a quick look at each.

In most states you must register your *company name* (also called a trade name) if the name is different from your own. Thus, you must register a name like Ace Products but you needn't register John Jones, Surveyor. I strongly recommend that you use a company name—it sounds better, you can derive more benefit from it, and the registration fee is nominal—usually less than $10.

Choose a specific name when you have a highly specialized product. Bernard Castro, founder of Castro Convertibles Corporation, began his business with a $300 loan. Today he employs more than 1,000 people, has 44 stores, and is still expanding. The name he chose for his firm is specific; it helps promotes the product for which Castro is famous.

If you're undecided about your exact business or product, choose a general name like Ace Products, Ace Industries, Ace Enterprises, etc. Substitute any word you wish for Ace. This might be your own name, the name of the street on which the business is located, etc.

Use your home address for your *business address* if you want to save money. If at all possible, I recommend that you use a different address—either a post office box (about $9 per year) or a mailing address (around $5 per month). When your home and business addresses are different, people believe that you have an office or factory and respect your business more. Also, you won't be bothered by having salesmen or job applicants calling on you at home.

Use your home phone for your business telephone number until you can afford a separate business phone. Few people pay any attention to the address at which a telephone is located if they can reach you by phone during the day. If you wish, you can hire a telephone answering service to handle your business calls. The cost of this is usually about $12 per month and up, depending on the city or town in which you live, and also on the number of calls you expect.

Have a *letterhead* and envelopes printed (about $15 for 500 sheets of high-quality letter paper and 250 envelopes). If you expect to make changes in the letterhead or plan to print small circulars, buy a low-cost hand-operated printing press (about $40). With a little practice you can easily turn out professional-grade circulars and letterheads.

Use the *files* and *record book* you prepared earlier. Store your catalogs, clipped articles, ideas, and observations in these.

Ten Ways to Use Your Action Base

Once you've established your business, use it. Don't allow it to languish and die. Here are ten important ways you can use your business for profit:

1. Obtain valuable catalogs and data
2. Get free subscriptions to trade magazines
3. Establish eligibility for association membership
4. Provide activity during unemployment
5. Build a record of top-level responsibility
6. Furnish employment recommendations
7. Improve your credit rating
8. Obtain easier access to important people
9. Improve your self-confidence
10. Increase your money-making ability

Let's take a quick look at each so you can apply every technique in your search for a quick fortune.

1. *Obtain valuable catalogs and data*: Write to companies, trade associations, the U.S. Government, and other groups on your letterhead and you'll get fast, positive results. Fill in and mail the "bingo" cards (new-product information) in the trade magazines covering your field and you'll receive many valuable catalogs, data sheets, and other information free of charge. Some of these catalogs are 300 or more pages in length. You can also obtain free consulting service if you wish. None of these services are easily available unless you have an established business name.

2. *Get free subscriptions to trade magazines*: Many controlled-circulation magazines (identified by the initials CCA or

BPA in the Statement of Ownership in the magazine) will send you a free copy of the magazine each month if your business is in the field served by the magazine. Each copy can provide you with valuable information on building your fortune. If you didn't have the business name you might have to pay $10 to $25 per year for a subscription to the magazine. And, as mentioned above, you can get the newest catalogs and product information by filling out and sending in the post free "bingo" cards in each issue of the magazine. The information in catalogs and brochures is often worth thousands of dollars to you.

3. *Establish eligibility for association membership:* Many trade associations, professional societies, and similar organizations require that you be employed in, or in business in, their main field of activity. If you aren't, you may be unable to join the organization as a full member. Since membership in such a group can be valuable in your fortune hunt, you should join. You will meet people in the business, receive important publications, attend informative meetings, and learn many valuable procedures. Having an established business name opens all these, and many more, opportunities to you.

4. *Provide activity during unemployment.* If you're working for someone else now, and intend to build your fortune through a big salary, stock options, deferred compensation, and similar benefits, you'll have trouble if you're fired or laid off. It's much easier to change jobs while you're working. An employed man, for various reasons, is much more desirable to a prospective employer than an unemployed man. But if you're fired or laid off you can use your business name as your employer during your period of unemployment. You are "employed" and, therefore, more desirable to a new employer. Many top-level executives use this technique while between jobs. It isn't dishonest because you can actually be doing profitable business, or trying to find business for your company, while you're unemployed. This is why I said earlier that even if you seek your quick fortune through a job, you stand to gain by establishing your own company. As Robert Louis Stevenson said, "Everyone lives by selling something."

5. *Build a record of top-level responsibility:* When you run your own company you're a big man—even if the business is

small. Why? Because you solve all the problems yourself—sales, inventory, manufacturing, personnel, etc. You can build your fortune in your business or you can pyramid the experience you obtain by writing a favorable resume when you apply for your next job. As the owner of a company, you are looked on as a valuable catch by another company looking for an aggressive, hard-driving man. You build a reputation for top-level responsibility that few other people can duplicate.

6. *Furnish employment recommendations:* If someone works for you and your company, you can furnish a recommendation when that person is looking for work. A good friend of mine hired a top-notch part-time accountant for his business. When the accountant decided to take a full-time job my friend gave him a glowing recommendation. The accountant obtained an excellent job. Later, to show his gratitude, the accountant gave a large amount of business to my friend. Both prospered.

7. *Improve your credit rating:* When you use OPM (other people's money) to build wealth, as you'll almost certainly have to, you'll need a good credit rating. If you've held a steady job for a year or more at a high salary, you probably can borrow up to $5,000 on your signature. If you want more money, you'll need a better credit rating than that provided by a job. Having a business of your own will up your credit rating by many points. Most banks will be willing to lend you more than $5,000 if your business has promise.

8. *Obtain easier access to important people:* As owner of your own company you can write to or call on big men—presidents, vice-presidents, and managers—and be welcomed because you may bring valuable orders. You don't have to beg for an interview. When you're welcomed you have more confidence. You make a better impression and have a much greater chance of getting what you seek—an order, a job, an interview.

9. *Improve your self-confidence:* With your own company behind you, your self-confidence soars. At long last you feel some true freedom. You see the possibility of getting away from the 9-to-5 grind, surly bosses, and absolute dependence on one paycheck. You become braver, more aggressive, more self-reliant, and more creative. No matter how you're trying to build your fortune,

you have a greater chance of hitting the big money quickly if you have more self-confidence.

10. *Increase your money-making ability:* Setting up a small business of your own gives you valuable experience. When you fill out the necessary forms, learn the various laws governing business in your state, and see what a business must accomplish to succeed, you increase your money-making abilities. The knowledge you acquire is valuable. Few people take the trouble to establish a business. That's why most people remain relatively poor throughout their lives. Today, right now, take the first step in forming your own business. Select a suitable name. Then take the other necessary steps—registration, address, letterhead, telephone number, etc. See how much you improve your money-making ability.

Begin Now—Put Your Dreams to Work

Actionize your search for wealth. If you just sit and dream you'll never earn the first dollar of that fortune. So get up now and do something. Put your dreams to work. Make your hopes come true. *Actionize your search for wealth.*

CHAPTER 4

Start Small—Grow Big—Fast

You want to get rich fast—
in three to four years...

Once you've acquired some wealth you can pause, look around, and decide what you want next—more wealth or more leisure. Fritz Lowe, who composed the music for *My Fair Lady,* chose leisure. He can now relax; he travels extensively, charters a big yacht in the Mediterranean, and says he'll never write another note because he has more important use for his time.

Your Capital is Limited

If you're like most beginning smart money wealth builders, you have little or no capital. You're what the bankers call "thinly financed". So you must start small. But if you're to become wealthy, you must grow big—fast.

With the right business or job you *can* grow big fast. Some of the people you'll learn about in this chapter grew so big so fast that they had more growth problems than business problems. For instance, Jay Monroe, inventor of the high-intensity Tensor lamp, grew so fast that he was losing $20,000 a year in stolen lamps. The security system in the lamp factory wasn't as good as he wanted it to be. Yet his business boomed—he could hardly meet the enormous demand for his handy, practical little lamp. Sales of his popular miniature lamps skyrocketed from $1,000 the first year to over $3-million in the fourth year. Today his security system is top-notch.

It's true that growing big fast gives you problems. But as long as you have the income you can overcome the problems. It's when you don't have the business that your problems become almost insurmountable. So if you want to prosper quickly you must have a highly saleable idea, product, or skill.

Don't allow limited capital to discourage you. Most small businesses and careers that grow fast start with hardly any capital.

Ben Ciscel started Gulf Aerospace Corporation with a brochure and one employee. Within 30 months he built a $500,000 aerospace electronics business.

James Keena started his Mac-Aire Aviation Corporation with one used Cessna 150 two-seater plane. He wanted to teach people how to fly. During his first month he logged only 20 hours of flying time. Within two years his fleet grew to 16 airplanes— 10 new Cessna 150s, two new Cessna 172s, a twin-engine Cessna 310, a twin-engine Piper Apache, and two Mooneys—a Master and a Mark 21. After two years he had 16 people on his payroll; a big difference from his first month when he was the pilot-instructor, mechanic, president, and secretary—all by himself. He spends only $7 a year on advertising, and his planes recently logged

1,800 flying hours in one month. This is a flying-time increase of 8,900 per cent in two years!

So ignore the merchants of doom who tell you, "It takes a million to make a million." They are dead wrong because a person with the right idea or skill can still hit it big in this great and growing world of ours. Jay Monroe was told not to market his Tensor lamp because people in the lighting business thought the little lamp would fail to catch on. Yet Monroe took what is called a "a crapshooter's gamble" and won—big.

Get Started—Market Your Ideas

Careful reading of the first three chapters put you on the starting line for your quick race to wealth. Now the starting gun is about to fire. Get set to go.

Boris Said, Jr. was, as he puts it, "dead broke" when, as a 30-year-old ex-sports-car racer, he heard of 40 acres of desirable land for sale for a downpayment of $2,600. Using all his ingenuity, he rounded up $251. Borrowing the remainder (see Chapter 6), he bought the land. Within six months he made a profit of $110,000 on 36 of the 40 acres. On the other four acres he built a new home for himself. Within two years after investing that $251, Boris Said, Jr. was a millionaire. How did he do it? The same way you will.

Boris Said Jr. believed he could subdivide his real-estate holdings so home builders could set any boundary lines they wanted —to include a brook, a tree, or favorite bushes. This was his idea. He bought the 40 acres to prove his idea. Buying the land was his start. Later he expanded his idea, buying 842 acres. His holdings became larger than the land occupied by a nearby village.

You can't build wealth by sitting and dreaming. You must start—no matter how small your beginning. Boris Said, Jr. started with only 40 acres—later he increased his holdings by a factor of more than 20 times.

Buy, lease, sell, market, or rent your idea, product, skill, or other commodity. If you can't spare time away from your regular job because you need the income, work in your spare time. See Chapter 11 of this book and all of my book *How to Build a Second*

Income Fortune in Your Spare Time, Parker Publishing Company, West Nyack, N. Y., for many profitable ideas and techniques.

Know Your Market

No matter what business or career you choose to build instant wealth, you'll have to sell something. That something might be yourself, a product, a service, or any of hundreds of other items. To sell effectively you must know your market.

What must you know about your market? At least seven facts:

1. The size of the market
2. The location of the market
3. The price range the market will accept
4. The main needs of your market
5. The product features most appealing to the market
6. The buying habits of the market
7. The principal members of the market (men, women, etc.)

Srini T. Srinivasan lives in a community populated by families having many cultural and educational interests. He studied the people in the area and found that they were interested in books, music, art, literature, and curios from all over the world (item 4, above). Further study showed that both the adults and children in the area would be interested in world-wide products (item 7).

For the children, prices must be moderate. Adults can afford more but they, too, might want certain types of products— for use as hostess gifts—at lower prices, under $5 (item 3).

Mr. Srinivasan made other studies of his market—size, location, needs, product features, etc. These indicated there was a need in his community for a store dealing in cultural items from worldwide sources. He selected a site and opened a book and gift shop named *The World and I.*

Today *The World and I* is booming. There is a steady flow of customers—adults and children—through its door. Mr. Srinivasan's idea is paying off because he analyzed his market, found a need for particular products, and met that need.

Two friends of mine are in the art business. One is partner in an art store—I'll tell you more about him in Chapter 6. The other friend is an electronics engineer who sells art—paintings, drawings, sculpture, etc.—to *his* friends. This engineer spends his weekends visiting friends who are interested in art.

The art-store partner sells the art to the engineer. "He's back every week," says the store owner. "I mark my prices up two to four times or more. The engineer buys at *my* price and sells at his. His markup is two to four times what he pays us."

"How does he do it?" I asked the store partner.

"He knows his market," was the answer.

This engineer has almost no operating expenses because he keeps the paintings in his car while waiting to sell them. His sales are sometimes as high as $1,000 per week—yet he spends less than a day a week at this work. He substitutes knowledge of his market—what people want and what they will pay for it—for long hours spent seeking sales prospects.

Learn the Job Market

Knowledge is power, is so true in quick fortune-building. You use your knowledge of a need to corner a market. Find one big need and fill it and you can become wealthy within weeks. Later chapters show you hundreds of ways to find, meet, and profit from the needs of your market.

If you seek your fortune through a job you must know your market, just as in a business of your own. For if you know what skills the market seeks, you can acquire them and fit yourself for a better paying job.

Tom L., in his middle forties, was a self-trained accountant who worked for a book publisher. On the side, Tom invested in the stock market. His investments were small because his salary at the publishing house—$8,000 per year—just about met the bills Tom and his family ran up. But Tom remained a serious student of the stock market, studying every good book about the market that he could obtain.

One day, without warning, Tom's boss told him that the accounting job was being eliminated. Tom had four weeks during which he could look for another job. After that he'd be out on the street.

Tom nearly panicked. With two children and a wife to support, a man in his middle forties can have real problems when trying to find a new position. Within a few days Tom calmed down. "What can I do?" he asked himself. The answer came to him the following night while he was on his way home. Tom decided that he would explore every possible industry in which an accountant might be needed. Until now Tom had thought only of getting a job in book publishing. For a reason he couldn't understand, Tom felt relieved and happy after he made his exploration decision. He didn't know it then, but what he really decided to do was to know his market—the market for his accounting skills.

The next Sunday Tom studied every employment ad in the biggest papers serving his city. He was amazed to note that the largest advertised salaries ($17,000 to $30,000 per year) were for security analysts. Also, there were a large number of ads for analysts, showing that there was a real need for them. The more ads Tom read, the more he realized that a security analyst combines a knowledge of accounting with a knowledge of the stock market. Tom thought he knew enough about both subjects to qualify as a security analyst.

The next day Tom borrowed several books on security analysis from his local library. He studied these and found that he had enough accounting and stock-market knowledge to obtain a job. He began his job search, concentrating on employment agencies because they could supply him with additional information about the job he sought. Within a week Tom had a job as a security analyst at $17,000 per year. Today, two years later, he's earning $24,000 per year. Thus, Tom was able to obtain a $16,000-per-year increase in his income in two years because he knew his market. Now Tom has his eye on a $30,000-per-year job. He'll get it, too. You can do the same if you analyze the job market for your skills.

Parlay Profitable Ideas

Mort Weisinger started to write an article on items that can be obtained free of charge by the public. He planned to title the article "Land of the Free." As he collected information for his article he began to see that he'd never have enough space to cover the hundreds of free and useful items. So he expanded his article into a book titled *1,001 Valuable Things You Can Get Free*. At the time of this writing, his book has sold more than 2 million copies.

What did Mort Weisinger do? He parlayed an idea with limited profits into an idea with almost unlimited profit potential. As time passes and new free products become available, Mort Weisinger will probably revise his book and publish a new edition. This will increase the sale of his book.

You probably have many profitable ideas you can parlay to wealth. The key is this:

To parlay an idea to quick wealth, look for a way in which a small beginning can be built to a major sale.

Don't allow your good, profitable ideas to die. Put them to work. Get every dollar of profit you can from your ideas. Then your wealth will grow quickly and steadily.

Sidney Solomons, a British dress designer, was having a pint in a London pub when a young man, Robert Benson, walked in carrying a fat, balloon-like red and white sewn-cloth head. The customers in the pub howled with laughter at the expression on the face of the stuffed head. Benson introduced the stuffed cloth head as Mac Gonk. He explained how Mac got his start. Benson sewed the head and face by hand then stuffed it with grated foam rubber.

Sidney Solomons was delighted with Mac Gonk and he borrowed the head to show his children and wife. Mac Gonk was welcomed with joy and immediately made a member of the family.

Within a short time, Mac Gonk was put to work. Gonks Ltd. was formed to market the Gonks. An entire line of stuffed heads was developed for children and adults. In a year London "went Gonk", with a whole line of products—jewelry, sweat shirts, dish cloths, dishes, knitted hats, slippers, and aprons. A Gonk cartoon strip is in the making.

Gonks are now on the American market. During their first month, 250,000 American Gonks were sold. The U. S. Gonk price is $5; the British price $8. Larger markets are expected as new Gonks are introduced.

Thus, Robert Benson and Sidney Solomons built one idea from a small beginning into a big, major product in less than two years. You can do the same if you stay constantly alert and if you are ready to parlay a profitable idea into a fortune.

Aim at the Big Money

Just because you start small doesn't mean you must remain small. James L. Hunt began his career as a fighter pilot, became an admiral in the U.S. Coast Guard Reserve, and went on to become the top-selling Chevrolet dealer in the United States. Entering real estate, he recently sold 1,140 home sites on land he improved by putting in roads, drainage, canals, and other facilities in what was once barren land. He sold these sites for $4 million in 8 minutes. Over 6,000 people showed up to take part in what Mr. Hunt calls his "land rush" sales.

J. C. Penney, founder of the huge store chain, began his business with only $500 in cash. By the time he was 45, Mr. Penney had 326 stores in 26 states. Now he has more than 1,700 stores selling to millions of customers.

How did Mr. Penney's business grow so fast? He concentrated on offering quality goods at modest prices to the largest market he could find. This wise decision led to the enormous growth of his small starting capital.

A Fortune on Your Job

If you want to build your fortune in a job, aim at the top-paying activities. Advertising is one of these. Salaries of $30,000 to $50,000 per year are commonplace in New York—advertising's center of activity. You can rise fast in advertising if you are creative and can produce ideas fast.

Harry Conover introduced the "Conover Cover Girl" to the advertising and publishing world. He started his business in a one-room office on which he spent $500 for furniture. Within ten years his office grew to a 12-room suite and his business grossed $2 million per year. Conover created the all-American, well-scrubbed, coed look in advertising and on magazine covers. He invented unusual and colorful names for his models—Candy Jones, Jinx

Falkenburg, ChooChoo Johnson, Chili Williams, and others. Mr. Conover combined creative ideas with a big-money business.

A man I know recently left his job as a mechanical engineer to take a job in a large department store. I thought I knew why he did this but I asked him, just to be sure.

"The highest pay for executives is in the department-store field," he said. "I ran a survey of executive salaries and decided I wanted to work where the big money is."

Here's a list of the top-paying industries in the United States. Use this list as a guide if you are seeking your quick fortune in a job. Go where the BIG money is!

INDUSTRIES PAYING HIGH WAGES TO TOP EXECUTIVES

(1) Large department stores
(2) Auto manufacturing
(3) Food manufacture and sale
(4) Chemical processing
(5) Steel manufacture and sale
(6) Computers and data processing
(7) Electronics and electrical equipment
(8) Aerospace and missiles
(9) Oil exploration and refining
(10) Airline operation

Some fortune builders vary this big-money approach. Instead of taking a position in a high-paying industry, they enter an activity in which they can quickly move to the top. From there they expand their activities. Stanton Sanson joined the Lincoln Hosiery Corporation at the age of 15. Within four years he was president and part owner of the corporation. From here, Mr. Sanson expanded his interests to include real estate, finance, transportation, and textiles. His fast rise gave him the capital and position which were helpful in the expansion of his business interests.

Seek—and Find—the Unexpected

Make *serendipity* (finding something good when you don't expect it) work for you. Put yourself in the place where *good* things might happen.

Kip Wagner and Lisbon Futch knew of the Spanish gold fleet that was wrecked by a storm on Florida's east coast in 1715. The ships were carrying treasure—gold and silver—estimated to be worth up to $14 million. Wagner and Futch spent years searching the beach and nearby waters for the wrecks. Recently they made their first big strike, bringing up more than 1,200 gold coins. At an auction one of the coins was sold for $3,600. About $50,000 was obtained for 107 of the coins—and there are more than 1,000 left to sell! Wagner and Futch sought—and found—a bigger treasure than they expected.

Of course, most of us can't go scuba diving off Florida's coast for wrecks of gold-laden treasure ships. But we can seek treasures elsewhere, in less dangerous areas and with greater chances of success. During years of watching people trying to *hit it big*, my main finding is that most folks never bother to find out about, and use, the *treasure* facilities available to them. Yet there are thousands of valuable opportunities available to all of us. We need only look around to find them. Let's take a quick look at a few of these *treasure* sources which can help you start small, grow big—fast.

Use Good Fact Sources

There's a monthly newsletter, *International Wealth Success*, P.O. Box 186, Merrick, N.Y. 11566, that is full of valuable listings of capital sources, good businesses for sale, excellent jobs (some paying as high as $100,000 per year), mortgages available, business partners wanted, etc. A recent issue carried listings for:

- 100 per cent financing at low interest rates
- Investments yielding 300 per cent annually
- Nursing Homes for lease
- Funds for real-estate financing
- Mail-order businesses for sale
- Guaranteed 100 per cent profit in cattle ownership
- Franchises of many types
- Oil-producing properties for sale
- Auto distributorships

- Ideas wanted for complete production runs
- Timberland and vacant land wanted
- Hundreds of finder's fees opportunities

Read this newsletter in the privacy of your home every month. Send for more information on the listings that interest you. If you are diligent in your search you will find your *treasure* without leaving your living-room. This is truly a treasure-hunter's paradise. A subscription costs $24 per year and is well worth it.

For $1.50 per year you can subscribe to a valuable United States Government report which is popularly known as the *Insider's Report*. This valuable report lists the stock transactions of officers, major stockholders, and directors who buy and sell the stock of their own firms. Many smart stock-market operators believe that the actions of insiders are a clear clue to the future trend of a company's stock. Thus, if an insider sells a large block of stock, this may mean the company is headed for trouble. Purchase of a large block of stock may portend good times ahead. Few people know better, these operators say, than the insider, what the future holds for a company. After all, the insider works in the company. Or if he doesn't, he has such large holdings—10 per cent or more—that he could.

Many shrewd stock operators, using little more than the *Insider's Report* and some borrowed capital, have made profits in the stock market. You might be able to do the same, using the report. To subscribe to the report, write to the Government Printing Office, Washington, D.C. 20402 and ask to be put on the mailing list for *Official Summary of Security Transactions and Holdings,* published by the Security Exchange Commission. Current subscription cost is $1.50 per year.

Find Big-Pay Jobs Fast

If you seek instant wealth through a high-paying job, investigate the executive-search and specialized employment agencies. There are many agencies in large cities which deal only in executive-level jobs—those paying $10,000 or more per year.

Find the names and addresses of executive-search and

specialized employment agencies in *The Wall Street Journal,* trade magazines serving the field you are interested in (Advertising Age, Textile World, Electronics, etc.), and your local large-city newspapers.

Some quick-wealth builders concentrate their efforts on the executive-search firms because they believe these firms have better jobs to offer. Since the executive-search firms seldom advertise, their efforts are usually secret. You stand a better chance of obtaining a good job when the need for a man is a confidential matter, known only to the employer and the executive-search firm. Another advantage of being "found" by an executive-search firm is that the employer always pays the fee—it doesn't cost you a penny to get the job, other than transportation and telephone charges.

To begin small and grow big—fast—on someone's payroll, send your resume to 100 or more executive-search firms. This will broaden your opportunities, opening new fields of wealth to you. For a comprehensive, classified directory of more than 200 top executive-search firms, write to ATC, P.O. Box 186, Merrick, N.Y. 11566 for *Executive-Search Firms.* The directory published by this company is regularly revised to include new executive-search firms and is well worth its $2.00 cost.

There are many other good sources of facts. You can obtain *Job Facts* and *Business Facts* at $2.00 each from the above publisher. These two publications list key sources of job facts and business facts. Most of the items are free, or you can read them free of charge at your local library.

Other good sources of facts include trade associations, professional societies (for example, The American Society of Mechanical Engineers), people in the same or similar business or job, business advisers, employment counselors, etc. Lastly, never overlook the value and importance of good books as a source of valuable information. You can, if you wish, begin to operate a business of your own, if you follow the suggestions given in this book.

Use the One-Product Technique

You are about to discover a technique which I believe is the fastest known for developing wealth from a small beginning. I've seen it used successfully by hundreds of successful quick wealth builders. Here, for the first time anywhere, is the essence of the *one-product technique:*

Find, develop, invent, or acquire a product, service, or other commodity which, when sold in small numbers, will bring you wealth.

The whole secret of the one-product technique is based on two simple facts: (1) multiplication, and (2) small numbers. Let's take a look at each.

Suppose you sold 1,000 items at $1,000 each. What would your total income be? Find it by simple multiplication, or (1,000) x ($1,000) = $1,000,000. Thus, by selling only 1,000 items you've grossed $1 million. If you were to sell these items in the United States where the population is close to 200 million, you would have to sell one item for every 200,000 people. Thus, you have a huge market.

The small-number feature of the one-product technique is in the number of units you sell to earn a big profit. In the above example you sold only 1,000 items to earn $1 million gross income; if you sold 5 items per day, you'd earn $1 million gross income in a year.

What would happen if you didn't sell 1,000 units? Suppose you sold only 500. What then? Your gross income would drop to $500,000. This is still more than many people earn in a lifetime.

You can't find a product or service that sells for $1,000? And you can't develop one, you say? Well, how about developing or finding a $200 product or service and selling 5,000 of it? Or look for a job in which your commission is several hundred dollars per sale.

You're not a salesman—you despise selling? Try another approach.

A man I know is a consulting management engineer. When he first went into business a few years ago, he charged his clients a daily fee for his services. But this engineer soon found that he was scrambling for daily fees. Clients were often late or slow in paying, leading to complex collection problems.

My friend became exasperated. He switched to an annual fee of $1,000 for 20 days work if the client required it. He soon found that most clients didn't actually use 20 days a year of his time, even though they signed up and paid $1,000 for the time. So he signed up 45 clients. His business and income boomed.

Today this engineer's standard retainer is $6,000 per year and he has 30 clients. Thus, his guaranteed income is (30) x ($6,000) = $180,000 per year. He is making full use of the one-product technique and his talents (Chapter 7).

I live in a town named after a branch of my family. This town, Hicksville, is on Long Island, in New York. For years, Hicksville and the county in which it is located, Nassau County, have been among the fastest growing in the United States.

Al Bianco, a top-notch insurance salesman, recognized this growth. After studying the situation for eighteen months, Al Bianco decided to found his own insurance company on Long Island. He raised $1 million in capital by selling 3,500 shares of stock at $300 per share. With this starting capital and one secretary, Bianco went into business.

During its first twelve months, Bianco's insurance company made $19 million in sales. In its second year, sales rose to $33 million; by the third year they were more than $50 million. Shortly thereafter they reached $100 million. The company, in less than 4 years, rose from a two-person staff and took its place among the top U.S. insurance companies. Within seven years, Al Bianco hopes to be selling $1 billion worth of insurance.

Thus, Al Bianco, by concentrating on one product—insurance—built a large business in less than four years. He is an example of how you can expand at an enormous rate if you specialize in one product for a growing market.

Start Small; Grow Big—Fast

Almost everyone who seeks wealth must start small because his capital is limited. Yet almost all of us want quick wealth. We hate to wait a lifetime for a big income because we sense that we may not have the physical vigor to enjoy the delightful flood of dollars. While we may think of leaving something for our children after we're gone, our main interest in instant wealth is what we can do for ourselves and our children with the money today. A new house, a bigger car, long vacation trips, a summer place on a lake—all these, and many more, attract folks to quick wealth.

You *can* start small, grow big—fast, if you use the techniques given in this chapter. Keep these eight key steps in mind; put them to use every day of the year:

- Begin today—market your idea or skill
- Know your market from A to Z
- Parlay profitable ideas into riches
- Aim at the big money
- Seek—and find—the unusual
- Use good fact sources
- Sell one product in a growth market
- Use these key steps in business or on a job

CHAPTER 5

Jump Into Billion-Dollar Markets

The world is changing.
All nations, and the people in
them, are becoming wealthier . . .

As a person's income grows, he and his family want more out of life. Where three years ago there was a market of 5,000 people for a product, today there is a market of 50,000 people for the same product. By next year the market might be 150,000 people.

You can cash in on the world's growing affluence by jumping into profitable billion-dollar markets. This chapter shows you —step by step—exactly how you can earn quick wealth in the many huge markets open to you.

Be Alert At All Times

Billion-dollar markets are of two types—the fad type and the steady type. We'll look at the fad-type first because it is the easiest for you to enter and build instant wealth.

Most fad-type billion-dollar markets grow fast—and die fast. But while they're alive they generate billions in income. You remember recent fad-type billion-dollar markets—hula hoops, skate boards, pop and op art, surf boards, comic books, motor bikes, power lawn mowers, initial license plates for autos, etc. Some fad-type markets survive and become permanent markets. If this happens—as with power mowers, motor bikes, comic books, etc.—your wealth can grow for years and years.

Suppose, however, the fad passes as it did for hula hoops, ouija boards, and similar items. What happens to you? If you get into the market early, using the techniques given in this book, you may make a fortune—fast. The very nature of the market, its short life, makes you work harder. You earn money faster. Once you have a pile, you can sit back and relax while waiting for the next billion-dollar market.

There's just one key secret that leads you to the magic wealth of billion-dollar markets. This secret is: *Be alert at all times.*

To cash in on billion-dollar markets you have to sense a trend before the crowd does. You must be in the marketplace with your product before your competitors arrive. Ford Motor Company, seeing the enormous increase in teenagers and young marrieds, developed an auto, the Mustang, for just this market. The car was an instant success, orders were so far ahead of production that people had to wait months to get a car.

Thus, Ford (1) was alert to a need (teenagers and young people are more interested in cars than any other population group), (2) developed a suitable product with attractive styling, popular transmission arrangements (four-on-the-floor, etc.), (3) marketed the product as widely as possible.

Six Steps to Billion-Dollar Markets

You can discover billion-dollar markets as they develop by following a six-step plan:

1. *Spend time with young people*—that's where the money is today. A recent survey shows that teenagers have more cash to spend than their parents. Try to learn what *new* sport, hobby, or skill interests these kids. The number of teenagers grows by about two million each year.

2. *Develop two or three serious hobbies*—you may find your big market in a spare-time interest. Leisure is growing throughout the world. More people have more free time than ever before. For instance, boating is a wonderful hobby on which American enthusiasts spend nearly $3 billion per year. There are many other hobbies in the billion-dollar class—golf, skiing, tennis, etc.

3. *Read a good daily paper every day.* Learn what's going on. Spot trends as they develop. The first mention of the European discotheque was in a popular daily newspaper. Alert American businessmen sensed a need for similar dance places. Some opened places of their own while others went into business supplying needed equipment. Everyone prospered.

4. *Subscribe to—and read—two popular magazines. Time, Newsweek, Life,* or *Look* are all useful and will help keep you up to date. And since many of today's billion-dollar markets are for mechanical, electrical, and related items, read *Popular Mechanics, Popular Science,* or *Science and Mechanics.* Each will help keep you posted on new and interesting items.

5. *Listen to what people say.* Hear them when they talk. If more than one person tells you about a new summer recreation area in your vicinity, check it out. You may be able to buy land or open a concession which will be highly profitable. So listen and learn.

6. *Observe—see—what goes on around you.* Don't walk around in a daze. Look at people. Notice the clothes they wear, what they're carrying. Get in touch with, and keep in touch with, daily life around you. Then you'll be better equipped to jump in on a new trend early in its popularity.

Seven Who Hit It Big

MOTORCYCLES AND MOTOR BIKES

Soichiro Honda always loved engines, motorcycles, and autos. So when he heard of some small gasoline engines for sale at the end of World War II in Japan, he quickly bought them and installed them on bicycles because he knew that people were desperate for cheap transportation. Within a few years he was producing over 100,000 motor bikes per year. Honda expanded to the United States and Europe, quickly cornering nearly half the market. What Honda sensed, and filled, was the world's need for fast, cheap transportation. Even today, Soichiro Honda notes, "Half the world is not even in the bicycle stage and the other half is just entering the motorcycle stage. This simply means that the market for motorcycles is unlimited." Mr. Honda is in an ideal spot to serve the needs of this billion-dollar market.

DELICIOUS HAMBURGERS

Two brothers, the McDonalds, saw the need for a top-quality, low-cost hamburger. They opened a drive-in store, McDonald's, in San Bernardino, Calif. Fifteen years later there were 705 drive-in restaurants in their chain selling 408 million hamburgers and cheeseburgers to hungry local people and travelers. Total sales were $129.6 million, with predictions of $315 million in a few years.

What are the McDonalds giving the public? Convenient, clean, modern stores serving excellent food at a bargain price—15 cents for a hamburger. Today McDonalds sells more than a million hamburgers a day. They also sell soft drinks, milk, and ice cream. McDonalds is one of the biggest users of the franchise system, about which you'll learn more in a few minutes.

GIFTS FOR ALL

Several years ago Bates Johnson had a problem many husbands face; he wanted to buy his wife a birthday present but couldn't decide what to buy. Bates finally decided to give his wife a gift certificate and leave the selection of the gift to her. To allow her variety in the choice of her gift, Bates Johnson tried to buy a gift certificate good at several stores. He found there was no such certificate. That's when he decided there should be such a gift certificate and he would provide it.

Bates Johnson formed Certificates, Inc., which features "The World on a String", a gift certificate good at a large number of stores. In his first three weeks in business, Johnson sold a gross volume of $26,000 in special certificates. He hopes to expand rapidly so that he can capture a large part of the $1.7 billion annual gift business in his area. Thus, Bates Johnson found a need and is filling it at a profit to himself while at the same time he helps other people solve their gift-buying problems.

BACKYARD BARBECUES

Ralph Olswang always loved the outdoor life: camping, hiking, fishing, cooking in the open. He enjoyed cooking outdoors so much that on weekends when he couldn't go camping in the woods he'd "camp" in his backyard, cooking meals for his family on a crude outdoor grill. The odor of the cooking attracted neighbors from all around who wanted to learn how to cook outdoors. Ralph Olswang sensed that there was an enormous market for lightweight outdoor barbecue grills. He set out to design and manufacture them.

Available grills were heavy cast iron, difficult to handle, and dangerous if dropped while still hot. Ralph Olswang switched to lightweight aluminum. He made one of his first grills from an aluminum blanket holder which he fitted with four legs and a charcoal holder. Soon he founded a company to manufacture the grills. As outdoor barbecues became more popular, Ralph Oslwang developed and marketed folding grills, round grills, electric fire igniters, and similar products. Alertness paid off for Ralph Olswang—it enabled him to detect a growing market. He jumped in early and made a fortune.

Did Ralph Olswang stop after developing his grills? No, he began to explore other parts of the backyard. Result: he invented a lightweight folding clothes drier which is still popular. He also developed many children's toys. Perhaps his most unusual product is an electronic catalyst used in kitchen ranges to remove cooking odors.

SUPERMARKET BONANZA

Henry Reichman, mentioned earlier in this book, saw supermarkets and shopping centers become major factors in the lives of Americans. So he decided to make shopping more interesting and less work.

Today he markets the game *Spell Cash*, developed by a midwest grocer. In a recent year Harry Reichman earned $10 million from this and other games. The grocer receives royalties and has earned nearly $1 million.

Another game Harry Reichman introduced is *Split the Dollar*. This was developed by a Russian refugee. Reichman followed with another game, called *Only 19*.

Harry Reichman made his first million after he was 55 years old. He did it by buying good ideas from others and marketing them. His motto is "There's no limit to how much a man can do or how far he can go if he doesn't care who gets the credit."

BOOKS FOR SUCCESSFUL PEOPLE

William J. Casey is the author of more than 30 books on business, taxes, laws, and real estate. He writes these books in his spare time, while he isn't handling his full-time work as a highly successful attorney. Bill Casey's books are the best I've ever seen. I've used many of them in my various business activities and they answer every question I have. Bill deserves the more than $2 million his books have earned in royalties. Why? Because businessmen responsible for billions of dollars of business are happy to pay for the well-written books presenting useful information which Bill Casey prepares.

SAILING ON SAND

John Schindler built several three-wheeled sand sailboats for his family. These boats are sailed on sand—giving all the thrills and fun of sailing, up to speeds of 75 mph. Yet the boats are safe and inexpensive.

Several people who saw these sand sailboats wanted one for themselves. John Schindler formed a company to make the boats. He is now selling the fast three-wheeled boats in many areas.

Get a Top-Paying Job

With a big job you earn big money. You can't expect to earn $50,000 or more per year as a shipping clerk, or at some other menial job. To get closer to a big income you must seek, and find, a top-paying job.

Recently, a friend of mine, who is a partner in an outstanding executive recruitment firm, mentioned while we were having lunch at the Four Seasons, that he had a $60,000-per-year job open for a company president.

"Tom," I said, "how does a person get to the place in life where a company will pay him sixty grand a year?"

"By job-hopping," he replied. "There are ambitious people who move from one job to another, always getting a raise in pay. Soon they're at the $50,000 level—then they move on to bigger money."

Thinking this over, I had to agree with my friend, the executive recruiter. Many people I know are job-hoppers. They move from one company to another every few years. One man I know moved from editor of a book publishing firm to president of another firm in the same business in four years. His salary (which was less than $10,000 per year as an editor) is now over $50,000 per year. During the four years he worked for three different companies holding these jobs: editor; general manager; vice-president; executive vice-president; president.

You, too, can job-hop to the big money if you know what you want in life. The problem most job-hoppers have is that they change jobs for emotional reasons (they don't like the boss; the coffee-breaks aren't long enough, etc.). If these people would concentrate on job changes for more money, they'd make much surer progress.

There are three approaches to job changes you can use. The first, which involves no change, is unsuitable for you because it fails to bring quick wealth. But you should at least consider the possibility of starting as an office boy or shipping clerk and, after thirty years, becoming company president. It can still be done and *is* being done. The only trouble is that it's a long, hard road with all sorts of dangers along the way.

Job Wealth Before Forty

Use the second approach if you're under forty. Here are its nine easy steps.

(1) Pick a profession or job (banking, securities analyst, etc.) which doesn't require a license for you to work at it. If you already have a profession or job you'd like to continue following, skip this step.

(2) Make a quick one- or two-week study of the profession or job at at your local or a specialized library. Learn as much as you can about your new skill as quickly as you can.

(3) Prepare a resume of your past work experience. Try to relate your future work with your previous work. Thus, if you worked as an auto mechanic and you seek to leap into a job as an automotive engineer, stress your knowledge of engines, ignition systems, etc.

(4) Go out and look for a job in the profession or field you've chosen. Use the executive job hints given earlier in this book.

(5) Keep searching. Use the ATC list of executive recruitment firms mentioned in Chapter 4.

(6) Once you have your job, learn which part of the organization pays the highest salaries. If it is a branch different from one you're in, apply for an immediate transfer. If you're asked why you want the transfer, be truthful and say you want to earn more money. There isn't any law which prohibits you from wanting to earn more money.

(7) Study job ads; stay in touch with the executive recruiters. Know how much other firms are paying their people for the work you are doing. If there is a large difference—say $50 per week, or more—inform your supervisor. He may not be aware of the variation in pay scales.

(8) Take immediate steps to job-hop to a higher-paying company if you can increase your salary by $25 per week or more.

(9) Continue job-hopping, increasing your salary at each move, until you reach the income goal you desire. Remember: *You are a more attractive job candidate when you're working for someone else, and you can usually command a larger salary increase by job-hopping than by staying put on one job.* This is the magic secret you apply in job-hopping.

Job Wealth After Forty

If you're over forty, you don't have as much time to spend working and job-hopping. This is when I recommend you use the third technique. Here it is.

(1) Select your salary goal—say $50,000 per year
(2) Study the job ads for work paying this salary
(3) Select three jobs you could do
(4) Study the job requirements at your library
(5) Prepare an attention-getting resume
(6) Send your resume to companies and executive recruiters
(7) Keep trying—you'll find what you seek

The success of this approach results from the action you take in the seven steps listed above. You are audacious enough to apply for a top job. If you're persistent, sooner or later you will find the job you seek.

Don't be discouraged by the "we-don't-hire-over-forty" myth. I know of thousands of companies, large and small, that will hire the *right man or woman* at any age between forty and sixty.

Get In On The Franchise Boom

One of the surest ways for you to jump into billion-dollar markets in a business of your own is by obtaining a franchise for a good product or service. The right franchise offers you many advantages, including

Small investment
Standardized product or service
Experienced guidance
Known trade name or trademark
Accurate income predictions

There are hundreds of franchise opportunities available to you in many different activities. These include food, laundry and dry cleaning, car wash, miniature golf courses, bowling alleys, billiard parlors, and many others.

Some McDonalds hamburger franchises, mentioned earlier in this chapter, do more than $500,000 per year in business. Profit usually runs 15 to 18 per cent of gross sales. Thus, with sales of $500,000 your profit would be $75,000 to $90,000 per year. Your investment? A small $12,500, or slightly more in some localities.

Suppose, though, you have only $1,000 to invest. What then? Can you still find a profitable franchise? Certainly! Get a copy of Harry Kursh's *The Franchise Boom: How You Can Profit In It,* Prentice-Hall, for many useful ideas on franchises of all types. You should also subscribe to *Modern Franchising* magazine so you can keep up to date on the latest in franchising techniques. Another useful source of ideas is *National Franchise Reports,* 333 N. Michigan, Chicago, Ill. 60601.

Deal with a reputable franchise agency and you will obtain excellent results. The big advantage of a franchise is that you receive mature and valuable guidance and advice—free of charge. There's no better way for you to start small and grow big, particularly if this is your first business experience.

Seize the Opportunity

You *can* jump into billion-dollar markets and earn a quick fortune. As a start, follow the golden, money-laden principles given in this chapter. But before you begin, think about these wise words of a wealthy man who built, and is building, several fortunes in a few years:

"Too many people," he observes, "waste time waiting for that one *big* idea, instead of putting their smaller ideas to work. So what if you earn only half a million dollars instead of a million? Your next idea may earn two million dollars! The important point is that you should be working on at least one project. For while you sit and dream, others will get out into those billion-dollar markets and make part of that wealth theirs."

Get started today. It won't cost you a cent to look around, observe, study, listen, and *hear* what the market is saying. Then get out and sell your idea, product, service, or skill to the hungry billion-dollar market. The results can be delightful and could make you a wealthy person in a short time.

CHAPTER 6

Use the Magic of OPM to Build Your Riches

For years I've watched men and
women become rich quickly . . .

And for years I've seen a key idea at work in their lives. This idea is so important, and it has seared its way into my brain so deeply, that I'll never forget it. The idea—which could be your magic, high-speed key to wealth, as it has been for so many others—is this: *Given an adequate amount of capital—$1,000 or more—the average man or woman who sincerely wants to become rich will build his fortune in two or three years.*

The Key to Wealth

Why is this a key idea with almost magical power? Because I've watched so many people build wealth quickly that I'm convinced that most folks have the know-how, the drive, the desire, the energy, needed to make a fortune. What almost everyone lacks is *CAPITAL*. Once a person obtains the needed capital he booms ahead to sound and quick growth of his fortune.

You probably are one of these potential fortune builders. You have the ideas, the drive, the desire, and the energy to build your riches quickly. If you didn't, you'd be reading another book. Since many people build wealth quickly once they have the capital, so can you.

Use the Magic of OPM

OPM—*other people's money*—is the magic live-wire secret used by almost every major wealth builder to accumulate capital. Why invest your money when you have everything else needed to build wealth—ideas, drive, desire, and energy? Or, just as important, how do you build a fortune in a business when you have everything needed except the capital? There's just one answer— OPM.

There are other, hidden advantages of OPM. When you borrow money to finance a wealth-building venture you work harder to pay off your debt sooner so the entire income will be yours. While paying off the debt you build a better credit rating. Should you ever need more funds in the future, they will be easier to obtain. If you have private financing—i.e. individuals lend you money—they will want to lend you more money so they can make a profit on your ideas. Soon you may have more cash available than ways to put it to work. But this is a situation I won't worry about because if this book can get you more cash than you need, I'm sure you'll find profitable ways to put it to work.

Make Money on OPM

Now we come to the golden door to wealth; the profit-laden entrance to unlimited, instant riches. You are about to learn the most important principle of your life; a principle that applies to every business from acorns to zebras in any location from Key West to Seattle, Capetown to Juneau. You can put this principal to work *today* and earn profits *today*.

For years this principle was the guarded secret of international wealth builders. Holders of the secret whispered it to their sons in darkened rooms. Some valued the secret so highly they never even revealed it to their sons. Yet this secret principle can open the glory of wealth to *any* man or woman within moments. Here is this all-powerful, secret principle which can magically magnify your wealth to make you a millionaire:

> **Make money on other's people's money. Invest borrowed money so it earns a large enough return to (a) pay off the loan while (b) paying you a profit.**

Expand Your Wealth

Now let's see how this marvelous wealth principle can be put to work in your life. I'll give you actual examples from the experiences of people just like yourself.

Jim K. bought an apartment house for $4,000 cash, which he borrowed from a bank. The total rental income from the apartment house is $7,400 per year. Expenses—taxes, repairs, water, heat, and mortgage payments—reduce the income to $3,200 per year, net. Out of this net income Jim has to pay $130 per month, or $1,560 per year to the bank to repay the $4,000 loan. His *money in fist* (MIF) is then $3,200 - 1,560 = \$1,640$, or more than $135 per month. This is the cash he has left after paying *all* expenses.

Look at that last number carefully. Jim is earning exactly $136.66 per month without investing a cent of his own! If he buys twenty such buildings (which is easy to do), his monthly income will be $(20)(136.66) = \$2,733.20$, while his annual income will be $(12)(\$2,733.20) = \$32,798.40$! Note the magic key: *This income is being paid to Jim because he invested other people's money at a higher rate of return than the money costs him.*

If you find this difficult to believe, I have another, even juicier fact for you. While Jim is (a) paying back the bank loan, and (b) earning a good profit, he is also paying for the building! Each month a few more bricks in that building become his. In a few years he can, if he wishes, sell the building at a sweet profit. All on OPM!

Are you still stunned? Consider the following possibility. If he sells the building at a profit after a few years—which he can almost always do—he can give the buyer a mortgage. This means he will receive monthly mortgage payments, plus interest, for doing nothing except dropping the check in the bank. All this on other people's money!

Use OPM in Any Growing Business

Is rental real estate the only business where this magic profit principle works? No—you can use OPM in any business, anywhere. Thus, if you're interested in a bowling alley, tavern, luncheonette, coin laundry, ice-cream parlor, etc., you can use this principle. I chose real estate as an example because this is one of the activities in which I've made good money. My friend, the art dealer, mentioned in Chapter 4, started his business on OPM. Today, only one year later, his income is enormous.

All you need do to earn a good income on OPM is to find one or more profitable going businesses with a required down payment equal to, or less than, the amount of cash you can borrow. To check out a business that interests you, fill in the blanks in the Profit Checklist below.

PROFIT CHECKLIST

1. Down payment required, $...................
2. True net annual profit, $...................
3. Annual loan repayment, $...................
4. Difference, (2-3), = MIF, $...................

Set some lower limit for item 4, the cash in hand. As a beginner, aim at an income of at least $100 per month from *each* business. As you gain experience and establish a higher credit rating, you can raise the required income to $500, and then $1000, per month for each business.

Wilbur Clark started his business career as an elevator operator, "advanced" to a dishwasher and bus boy. But menial jobs didn't stop him from achieving his goal in life—quick wealth. With $2,100 in borrowed money he bought a cocktail tavern with a legal game room in the rear. *Within one year Wilbur Clark owned eleven taverns, each named after himself, and each financed on OPM!*

From this modest beginning Wilbur Clark went on to build the *Desert Inn,* one of the most famous inns in Las Vegas. He branched out to race horses and a racing stable. Four of his horses were *Buy In, Sell Out, Dead Broke,* and *Dumpty-Humpty.* Always an enthusiastic golfer, he built a million-dollar golf course. Clark didn't stop there—he expanded into real estate and oil. He is just one of thousands who, by using OPM to buy a *going* business, became enormously wealthy, quickly.

Start a Business Using OPM

"I'm not interest in buying a going business—I want to form my own business," you say. Fine—use OPM. It will work for you the way it has worked for thousands of others. Simply use the same Profit Checklist as outlined above, but base your cash in hand, Item 4, on *estimated income.*

There is one problem you may have when using OPM to start a business. Sometimes your *actual* profits will be much lower than your *estimated* profits and you will have trouble repaying your loan. That's why I recommend that you buy a *going* business for your first venture using OPM. It is easier for you to check out a going business to determine its exact income. There's less danger of the actual income falling below your estimates and you will be able to repay the loan and still have some cash in hand.

Two Outstanding Examples of OPM

One of the most creative uses of OPM was that devised by an ambitious young law clerk. His employer wrote a book on corporate finance and wanted to have it published. The 22-year-old law clerk, Richard Prentice Ettinger, convinced a printer to print the book on credit—$710 worth. That was the beginning of Prentice-Hall, Inc., today one of the world's largest book publishers. In a recent year P-H, as it is known in the book trade, sold more than $63-million worth of books throughout the world. This is one of the greatest examples of the power of OPM—from $710 of borrowed money to $63 million in business.

A. P. Moeller became a shipping millionaire, owning nearly 100 of the most modern ships. He branched out to shipyards, factories, chemical plants, and enormous holdings in East Africa. How did A.P., as he is called, start? As a relatively poor boy who borrowed money to start his first shipping line. Like Walter Bagehot, A.P. believes "The great pleasure in life is doing what people say you cannot do."

Get Set for Financial Success

Up to this point you've been getting your mind set to use OPM. You've been learning how you can use borrowed money to build a large, quick fortune. Several examples from the lives of others prove that you, too, can use this magic technique.

Now you're ready to learn how *you* can borrow OPM to build *your* fortune. There are many, many ways to borrow money. The more you know about these methods, the easier it will be for you to obtain the money you need to build a large fortune quickly.

How to Obtain Capital Without a Credit Rating

Let's use the *worst-case principle* to explore ways you can obtain capital without a credit rating. I'm not saying *you* find it impossible to obtain credit—we're talking about Mr. Worst Case. He's a guy who really needs help. All of us can learn something from his experiences.

Mr. Worst Case needs what for him is a large sum of money —say $15,000 to buy a billiard room that is currently showing a profit of $20,000 per year. The price of the billiard room is $25,000, but Mr. Worst Case needs only $15,000 for the cash down payment. He goes to a bank and asks the loan officer for a $15,000 loan. He tells the loan officer all about the business; its current income; future prospects, and the excellent calibre of its customers.

The loan officer listens intently until Mr. Worst Case is finished. Then the loan officer asks some questions. They are:

Does Mr. Worst Case have a savings account in this bank?

Does he have his checking account in this bank?

Does he have his safe deposit box in this bank?

Does Mr. Worst Case have any collateral to put up?

Does he have a credit rating at this or another bank?

Mr. Worst Case answers *no* to each question. As the loan officer continues to ask questions, Mr. Worst Case slowly begins to realize that his chances of obtaining the loan are nil. Finally, the loan officer says, "I'm sorry, sir. We like to make good loans. But you don't do business with us regularly. You don't have a credit rating at this or any other bank. Therefore we can't lend you the $15,000."

Mr. Worst Case is determined to buy that billiard room. He goes from one bank to another, improving his story and presentation at each. But without a credit rating, and with almost no banking record, he fails to obtain the money. Someone else buys the lucrative billiard room and begins a climb toward riches.

How could Mr. Worst Case obtain a loan? How could any man in a similar spot obtain a loan of this size? He could, if he had time and money, open checking and savings accounts in the bank. With this as a start, Mr. Worst Case could borrow a small sum—say $500—and repay it quickly—say in two months. By taking and repaying a series of loans in increasing amounts, Mr. Worst Case could build a strong credit rating with a bank in a year to eighteen months.

But Mr. Worst Case, like most ambitious wealth builders, doesn't want to waste time. He wants to buy that billiard room *now* so he can begin building riches immediately. What can he do? How can he get a loan if every bank refuses him and he doesn't have any friends or relatives willing to lend him money? There is one little-known but startling golden key to his money problem that he can use, you could use, and I do use—the *compensating balance*.

You can borrow money from companies, small banks, and individuals, for deposit in another bank as *collateral* for a loan you obtain from that bank. The collateral is called a *compensating balance* and you are not allowed to withdraw it. Why can you borrow money for a compensating balance while you cannot borrow a similar sum to invest in a business? Because when you borrow money for a compensating balance the money *must* be deposited in a bank for this purpose and the lender knows exactly where the money is. So he's willing to take a greater risk than a bank or individual.

Six Steps to Obtaining OPM

Now let's see how Mr. Worst Case can finance his billiard room or any other business using this golden technique. He takes these six teps:

1. Obtain $15,000 compensating balance
2. Deposit compensating balance in savings account at bank
3. Give passpook to compensating-balance lender as collateral
4. Borrow $15,000 from bank using compensating balance as collateral
5. Buy billiard room with $15,000 down payment
6. Use billiard-room profits to pay off $15,000 loan

Thus, Mr. Worst Case finances his business without investing a penny of his own. Where can you find organizations and people interested in lending money for compensating balances? Here are typical sources; refer to the Business Opportunities and Capital Available columns of each:

The Wall Street Journal
The New York Times
The Los Angeles Times
The Chicago Tribune
The Houston Post
The Dallas News
The Miami Herald

Are compensating-balance funds free? No! Just like everything else in life, it costs money to borrow money. But the cost is low—three-quarters of one per cent per month is a typical cost. To offset this cost you'll receive 4 per cent, or more, interest on the compensating balance funds deposited in the savings account. What's more, the loan you make at the bank will be at a lower interest rate because you have full collateral.

Other Uses of a Compensating Balance

Let's say Mr. Worst Case needed only $3,000 cash immediately but might need an additional $12,000 within the next few months. He could use his compensating balance to set up a *line of credit*—i.e. the bank would allow him to write checks for sums up to $15,000 for business purposes. Some banks will allow you a line of credit up to 80 per cent of the compensating balance. With a $15,000 compensating balance this would be 0.80 (15,000) = $12,000 line of credit. Other banks will grant a line of credit up to 100 per cent of the compensating balance. Check the banks in your local area to determine their practices.

With a compensating balance the vice-president of any bank will welcome you when you apply for a loan. He'll ask only two question—(1) How much money do you have for the compensating balance? (2) How much do you want to borrow? So long as (2) is less than, or equal to, (1) you won't have any trouble.

Other Ways to Borrow OPM

Don't limit yourself to compensating-balance loans. Investigate:

(1) Mail-order loans
(2) Credit-union loans
(3) Finance-company loans
(4) Homeowner loans
(5) Public stock offering

Let's take a look at each. We'll assume that you have the four answers for the Profit Checklist we presented earlier.

1. *Mail-order loans* are available to almost everyone having a regular income. Obtain a recent issue of *Popular Mechanics, Popular Science,* and *Science and Mechanics.* Study the Classified Advertisements in each. You'll find several mail-order loan firms advertised. Send a postcard requesting a loan application.

Some mail-order firms will lend you up to $800 for two years; others will lend up to $2,500 for the same period. The amount depends on the state in which the mail-order firm is located.

Once you've acquired some solid business experience you

can consider taking out several mail-order loans to finance an investment. Thus, with three $2,500 loans you'd have $7,500 to invest in a business. In general, a sum of $5,000 or more will permit you to take your pick of a good business to buy. Thus, OPM obtained by a mail-order loan can put you on the road to fast riches.

2. *Credit-union loans* are a popular way to raise money for worthwhile investments. You can join a credit union where you work, where you live, in a fraternal organization, or in a similar organized group. There are some "open" credit unions— i.e. credit unions anyone can join. Such credit unions can be par- ticularly valuable to you if there isn't a credit union where you work.

Most credit unions will allow you to borrow one month's salary or $750, whichever is less, on your signature without col- lateral. To borrow larger amounts you need co-signers—relatives or friends who will take over your loan if you fail to pay. With co- signers you can borrow an amount equal to the sum of your monthly salary plus that of the co-signers. Thus, if you earn $700 per month and you have two co-signers who earn $2,000 and $1,800 per month respectively, you can borrow $700 + $2,000 + $1,800 = $4,500.

A big advantage of a credit-union loan is the low interest rate; only one per cent of the unpaid balance per month. This is a lower interest rate than you can obtain from most banks unless you use a cash compensating balance or some other form of collateral —stocks, bonds, etc.

3. *Finance-company loans* may be your answer if you need money in a hurry to close a business deal. Amounts available vary from $800 to $2,500, depending on the state in which you reside. As with mail-order loans, you can put several finance- company loans together to obtain a larger amount. Don't do this, however, until you have some good experience in evaluating busi- nesses offered for sale.

The interest rate charged by finance companies is higher than that charged by banks or credit unions. But in general, you can obtain money easier from a finance company than from any other source. So if you don't have a credit rating, or have had financial problems in the past, welcome the services offered by a finance company. You'll pay a few more dollars in interest. But wouldn't you rather hit it big while paying that higher interest than miss your chance at quick wealth while saving a few dollars in interest? I've always felt that the cost of interest was insignificant compared with the opportunities it opens to the competent fortune builder.

4. *Homeowner loans* are available to people owning one or more homes. These loans range up to $10,000 or more, and can be paid off in five years or less. The five-year pay plan is longer than you can get from a bank or finance company for a personal loan. Here's one five-year payment schedule you might use:

YOU BORROW	YOU PAY PER MONTH
$ 1,000	$ 21.25
$ 2,000	$ 42.50
$ 3,000	$ 63.75
$ 4,000	$ 85.00
$ 5,000	$106.25
$ 6,000	$127.50
$ 7,000	$148.75
$ 8,000	$170.00
$ 9,000	$191.25
$10,000	$212.50

You can also use an *interest only plan*. With this arrangement you pay only the interest on the loan for 59 months. The sixtieth payment is the full amount of the loan, plus the interest for that month. The usual interest cost is $8.33 per month per $1,000 borrowed for any period up to five years. The final payment is called the *balloon* or *bubble* payment.

If you want, you can obtain first or second mortgages on property you own. Some mortgage companies will lend up to 90 per cent of their appraised value on your property. Thus, if your your property is appraised as worth $20,000, you can borrow 0.90 ($20,000) = $18,000. Your monthly payment would be $128.96 for 20 years.

Some mortgage companies use a *standing* mortgage—you pay only interest until the final payment is due. Then you pay the full amount of the loan. Other companies use a partial standing mortgage—you pay interest plus a portion of the principal. Here are typical payments for three-year second-mortgage partial standing loans:

YOU BORROW	YOU PAY PER MONTH	BALANCE DUE AFTER 36 MONTHS
$ 1,000	$ 15.00	$ 723
$ 3,000	$ 45.00	$2,190
$ 5,000	$ 75.00	$3,617
$10,000	$100.00	$9,325

Does the balance due after 36 months frighten you? Are you worried about paying high interest rates? If your answer to both these questions is *yes*, then you're not ready to use the magic of OPM to build your fortune. To test your readiness for using OPM I've planted another little test in the above paragraphs. Enter your answers to the following questions:

1. High interest rates cheat me   (Yes or No) ....
2. High taxes will rob my profits (Yes or No) ....

If you answer yes to both questions, concentrate on building your fortune on a job. With one yes and one no, read on. There are three secrets you must learn.

THE SECRETS OF OPM

(a) All interest is tax deductible—so you have a legitimate, provable tax deduction every time you pay a dollar of interest.
(b) There are many legal, provable business deductions you can use to reduce your taxes.
(c) If, at the end of 36 months, you can't repay the balance due, you can refinance. Many smart money fortune builders refinance their loans over and over again. They believe that the interest cost is insignificant compared with the opportunities building a fortune gives them. Some even lend money and collect interest *after* they've made a fortune.

5. *Public Stock offerings* can get you cash for building a quick fortune. Two friends of mine, Meredith G. and Mel P., recently raised $200,000 in cash through a private offering of the stock of their newly formed corporation.

You must have a corporation if you wish to sell stock to the public. The cost of forming a corporation varies between about

$100 and $500, depending on the state in which you incorporate. Always use a lawyer when having the corporation papers prepared. You will pay a few dollars for legal fees but you will get every penny back in advice and service.

You can do much of the work of preparing a public offering yourself. Buy or borrow a copy of the excellent book by William J. Casey, *How to Raise the Money You Need to Start, Run or Expand a Business,* Institute for Business Planning, and follow its directions. If you use a Regulation A offering you can obtain up to $300,000 tax free for use in your business.

With public funds for your business you must work hard to earn a good profit for your stockholders. This incentive will spur you on to earn a bigger fortune faster.

OPM and Your Job

There isn't too much OPM to be obtained by working for others. But if you have a job it's much easier for you to borrow from banks, credit unions, finance companies, etc. So never quit a job until *after* you've borrowed any money you might need. Better yet, don't quit a job until after your new business is earning a big profit.

Some companies offer their key employees stock options— a right to buy the company stock at a price lower than the current market price. If you're in this choice spot, go to your broker and ask for a loan covering the number of shares you wish to purchase. Sign a pledge promising to turn the shares over to the broker as collateral for the loan. Then work as hard as you can to pay off the loan.

Sometimes your employer may be willing to lend you money for a noncompetitive business. If you ever have such an opportunity, grab it. Never refuse such a generous offer. Many great fortunes have started with friendly financing like this.

Learn the Other Side of OPM

By now I hope that you're enthusiastically planning on applying for some OPM tomorrow. Good. I know that you'll be successful in your search. But let's stop for a moment and do some hardheaded business thinking.

You've made plans for the investment you intend to make. You know the profit potential and how you'll pay for the business out of earnings. But suppose the business fails? What will you do? How will you pay off the loan?

Sit down at your desk as soon as you finish this chapter and figure

(1) How I'd pay off the loans if the business failed
(2) How much money I'd have left to live on
(3) What a business failure would mean to my credit rating
(4) How soon I could start on a new venture

Only when you can answer these four questions should you start to use the magic of OPM to build your riches.

CHAPTER 7

Mine The Secret Wealth of Your Skills

Everyone—you, your friends, your relatives, business asso-ciates—has unique skills . . .

These skills are the result of your training, experience, and background. Thus, if you were born on a farm in the Midwest, your background is different from that of a person born in a large Eastern or Western city. Your education is somewhat different because courses and teachers vary from one locality to another. And, certainly, most of us have unique experiences in life; experiences that set us apart from everyone else in the world.

92

The combination of these three elements—your training, experience, and background—make up your skills. In this chapter you'll learn how you can mine the secret wealth of your skills to build quick wealth.

Tally Your Skills

Most people think of skills in formal terms; saying that an accountant, engineer, lawyer, or medical doctor is skilled. True, all these persons are skilled. But what about a chef, sword swallower, writer, artist, and song writer? Aren't these people skilled? Yes, they are. But there's one important difference between the first and second group of skilled people. The first have undergone years of specialized schooling while most, or all, those in the second group are usually self-trained.

So avoid saying "I don't have any skills; I never went to college." Who cares whether you went to college? In my work I hire many people. I employ people for one purpose; to do a better job than the competition. If you come to me looking for work I have only one question in mind: "Do you have the skills I'm looking for?" If you do, you're hired; if you don't, I'm sorry—try somewhere else.

List your skills in the space provided below. Include everything you're good at; be it a skill that earns money or just passes the time. (Some people are better at their hobbies than they are at earning a living).

MY SKILLS TALLY

1. ....
2. ....
3. ....
4. ....
5. ....
6. ....
7. ....
8. ....
9. ....
10. ....

Evaluate Your Skills

Which skills can earn money for you? Of these, which can earn the largest amount of money in the shortest time?

Merwin K. tallied his skills and found he knew more about frozen pork bellies, from which bacon is made, than any other subject. Deciding to try to earn a profit from this knowledge, he invested a small sum in the pork belly futures market because he knows the thinking of pig farmers, feed-lot managers, and packing-house owners. He bought ten futures contracts in March at $30.30 and sold them in August at $46.75 per 100 lb, for a profit of $48,000 in seven months! This shows you what even the most undignified-sounding skill can do for you when put to work. It is also an excellent example of the magic of the smart-money wealth-building techniques you are acquiring in this book.

Pinpoint your three best skills, listing them in a 1-2-3 order of profit potential thus:

PROFITABILITY POTENTIAL OF MY SKILLS

1. .... (Most profitable)
2. .... (Next most profitable)
3. .... (Third most profitable)

You now know your three greatest potentials. No longer need you vacillate from one skill to the next, doing a little here, a little there, wasting your energy because it is undirected. You are ready to zoom off to a quick fortune, using the wealth potential of your unique skills.

Put Your Skills to Work

Thomas Kline started work at the age of twelve for $5 per month. Among his skills was a good knowledge of the local river, its currents, tides, and weather conditions. One winter the river froze over in November, trapping cargo ships laden with food and other valuable cargoes. Ship owners and merchants panicked because they thought the ships would be trapped all winter. Not one of them could remember such an early solid freeze of the river.

Thomas Kline remained calm. He bought three small ships for practically nothing and loaded them with food, using borrowed money to finance his purchases. Then he waited for what he knew would happen—quick melting of the ice. That night the ice melted; the next morning Kline sailed his three ships to a nearby port where he sold his cargoes for a $50,000 profit! Kline used his skill, knowledge of the river weather, to earn a quick, large profit. From this beginning Kline went on to build a multi-million-dollar fortune based on his skills.

Clint Pearson is a skillful yachtsman. He knows boats and people who have boats. Using this knowledge, he began building 8-foot glass fiber dinghies in a garage. All boatmen have trouble with wooden dinghies; they leak, peel, crack, and get numerous bangs and gashes. Every boatman wants a trouble-free dinghy; one he won't have to caulk, sand, paint, and repair. Clint Pearson aimed at this large market.

Soon he was building big glass fiber sailboats—the Triton was an instant success, selling more than 500 at about $10,000 each. (See Chapters 4 and 5 for the principles at work.) He sold shares of his company to the public (Chapter 6) and later sold 80 per cent control of the company to what is now Grumman Allied Industries. Today Pearson has his own company, Bristol Yacht Company, again. His biggest boat today is a beautiful 42-footer which is finding wide acceptance among the yachting public.

Gertrude Ford Ramsay loves tea. She also believes in success. Because, as she says, "For everyone in the world there is a good living to be made. But we must choose one thing and stick to it. Concentration on one ideal, one profession, or one article of trade will bring success."

Looking for a product having a steady need, Gertrude Ramsay decided that blended tea would go over well. For two years she experimented with different blends. Founding the Ford Tea Company, she sells quality teas to hotels, restaurants, and clubs. One of her big innovations is the tea bag, which allows easy and sanitary preparation of a cup or pot of tea. Her teas are a favorite throughout the world. Even the Duke of Windsor took some of it to England.

Paul Boretz is a skillful collector of businesses. Starting as a clerk, he gained control of a large and profitable bank. From this he went on to an empire composed of steel companies, department stores, and finance companies. Some years later, Boretz opened a tiny book business. Soon he built a new chain of 20 bookstores, two magazines, a printing firm, and a publishing house. Later in his life, Paul Boretz sold his publishing chain. But he didn't give up collecting businesses. Soon he controlled a group of cleaning companies. His various holdings are estimated as worth more than $150 million.

Claud Foster remarks, "Everything I touch turns to money." And it's true. The son of a poor farmer, Foster invented a shock absorber for automobiles that earned him millions of dollars.

Claud Foster has always had one skill; he can think up different ways of doing things. He also believes that God is his secret partner in his inventions and success. At the age of fourteen he decided that he could plant potatoes before the winter frosts ended. After much discussion, his father allowed Claud to plant four acres of potatoes. The early potatoes sold well and Claud Foster paid off a long-standing debt of $1,800 that had worried his father for years.

Teaching himself to play the trombone, Claud invented a musical horn based on an idea he got from an automobile exhaust. Founding the Gabriel Manufacturing Company, Claud Foster made $150,000 from the sales of the Gabriel Horn before he sold the company. Then he went into the shock-absorber business, basing his design on the way a boat is snubbed into a dock by a rope wrapped around a bollard. This idea brought him $1-million a year for many years.

Today Claud Foster gives his money away to hospitals, schools, orphanages, and his employees. At a recent meeting he donated $4-million to educational, charitable, and medical funds. "Too many institutions get their money from dead men," Claud Foster said. "I wanted to see them get it. I have no more use for the money."

What did these five fortune builders do that many other

skilled people don't do? Each of these intelligent fortune builders put his skills to work. He sought a way or ways to turn his skills into a fair profit. You can do the same. Here's how.

Turn Your Skills into Profits

Every skill has one or more buyers. But you don't want just *any* buyer. You want:

1. The *largest number* of buyers; those
2. *Buyers* who will pay *your price*
3. *When* you want to sell
4. Under conditions you believe are *fair*
5. And at a *profit* which will build your fortune

An anxious, hungry man makes sales—but at the buyer's price. A relaxed, confident man sells at *his own* price and earns a handsome profit. That's what you want to do.

Sometimes your greatest selling skill is patience; a willingness and ability to wait for the *right* buyer or buyers to come to you for the skill you offer. You can develop a willingness to wait if you're reasonably sure you'll make the sale.

A friend of mine sells boats priced from $5,000 to $50,000. Recently I mentioned to him that he had a large number of unsold boats in his yard. "Yes," he laughed, "But they all seem to sell if you're willing to wait."

The ability to wait comes from having enough money on hand so you don't suffer while waiting for a sale. Use OPM (Chapter 6) when you're sure you can make future sales. But if you're just beginning and you're uncertain of how many sales you'll make, try using your own capital. Then you won't go into debt while you're waiting for the first big sale of your talent.

Remember that you may have to give some free service before you begin earning money from your skills. My first spare-time teaching experience was free instruction of college students who had failed a difficult course. The students did so well in the course that I was soon earning $5 per hour teaching in my spare time. Today my rate is $50 per hour. People come to me asking me to teach a course. Thus, I'm relaxed and confident. And the more relaxed and confident I am, the more people come to me requesting that I teach.

Five Steps for Making Profits from Your Skills

Here are five valuable steps for earning higher profits from your skills. Most of these steps can be used in either a job or a business. Start using as many of these steps as you can today and your profits from your skills will rocket ahead.

STEP 1: PUBLICIZE YOUR SKILLS

Use any legitimate means to inform people that you are a skilled worker with superior talent. Thus, you can (a) contribute your skills free to a good cause in your community, house of worship, youth group, etc.; (b) write short or long articles for a magazine or paper serving your field; (c) give free or paid lectures on your skill to groups listed in item (a); (d) consult for and with others on the details of your skills, their successful application, typical problems, etc.

Never undervalue publicity. James Drake is a leading dealer in rare books. Yet he always manages to find time to advise important rare-book collectors, libraries, universities, and schools on the formation of their rare-book collections. His readiness to give impartial, expert advice enhances his outstanding reputation in the rare-book field and contributes to his firm's business.

STEP 2: EXPAND YOUR SKILLS

Never sit on your hands, satisfied that you're sure you know *everything* about your skills. We can all learn, *and re-learn*. As time passes, new techniques are developed. Learn the new, the different, the unique. You will expand your skills while increasing your profit-making potentials. Update your skills by taking courses, reading the best magazines in your field, reading new books on your specialty, and by attending meetings of professional or trade groups in your field.

Wilfred J. Funk, the famous lexicographer whose monthly column, "It Pays to Increase Your Word Power", runs in *Reader's*

Digest, constantly studied words, their origin and meaning. This regular expansion of his skills enabled him to produce a steady and growing output of articles, books, word lists, and similar important and valuable contributions. His list of the ten most beautiful words —*chimes, dawn, golden, hush, lullaby, luminous, melody, mist, murmuring, tranquil*—is widely accepted and often quoted.

STEP 3: USE YOUR SKILLS

The quickest way to ensure profits from your skills is by using them; regularly, fully, and actively. Thus, you earn profits while improving and reinforcing your skills. The quickest way to lose your skills is by *not* using them. Thus, you lose in two ways; your skills dull and you have no income from them.

"But," you say, "my skills are so unique I haven't found a buyer for them for the last five years." This is unfortunate, but it's much more unfortunate if you haven't used your skills for the last five years. This may be one of the reasons why you haven't been able to find a buyer for your skills.

Never allow your skills to dull! Work for free, even for just a few hours per week, to keep your skills sharp and up to date. Practice at home, while you travel, at work; any place where you won't disturb people.

Edmund Tabell entered the investment business when he graduated from high school. Several years later, when business declined, Tabell left the investment field to become an actor. While rehearsing for his first show he continued his interest in the stock market. He left the theatre and returned to the investment field when his first son was born. Today Ed Tabell is recognized as the leading point-and-figure chartist on Wall Street. His salary is in the $100,000-per-year range because all his life he has used his unique skills.

STEP 3: PLAN FOR THE FUTURE

Your skills may be paying you a comfortable income today. But will they bring you a fortune tomorrow? They may, if you plan for the future. The man with a plan wins more success and a larger fortune than the man who just drifts from one task to another. Plan for the future and you can almost guarantee success.

Fred T., and I were enjoying after-dinner cigars at a table on a huge ocean liner headed for Europe. Several other businessmen were at the table. Someone began a discussion of business success and soon we all joined in.

"I was thinking just yesterday," Fred said, "that every time I planned something in business, the plan worked and I made money. But when I didn't plan, when I let things happen to me without trying to control them, I had trouble."

Everyone at the table instantly nodded in agreement. "That's sure true," remarked a southern businessman. "I agree one hundred per cent," said a Chicago-based salesman. "I plan every move I make," a New York businessman said.

Later, thinking over this discussion, I recognized that I, too, could say much the same. Every time I planned a business activity I made money. Some years ago I decided to write a series of books. I planned my time, my energy. The book you are reading now is the tenth published. Each is a financial success. Part of the income from the books is being put into planned investments; stocks, real estate, consumer products. These, too, are paying off because they are *planned*.

To plan effectively, choose a *date* by which you will achieve a desired *income* level using specific *skills* you now have, or will acquire. Thus, your plan covers the timing, (date), return (income), and means (skills) that you have in mind. Don't proceed with any business or job plan until you've studied each of these three factors. Then your chances for building a big fortune quickly will expand immensely.

STEP 5: PURSUE PROFITS EVERYWHERE

"Some of my best sales are made on the golf course," remarks a $100,000-per-year salesman. "I hardly ever close a sale in the office—there are too many interruptions from telephones, secretaries, and visiting firemen."

One party I attended returned $2,000 in two minutes! I was talking to a man about writing (Step 1) and mentioned that I teach technical writing to groups of engineers and scientists. "You do!" he said. "How about teaching our engineers?"

"I'd be glad to, if the fee is right," I said.

"We pay $50 per hour," he said.

"You have a teacher," I told him, and we shook hands. I gave two 20-hour courses at his company and expect to give several more.

The more I see of modern business the more I realize how many deals are made away from the office, at lunch, during non-business hours, and at other odd times. Trammell Crow, who estimates his personal net worth as about $15-million, met Storey Stemmons, a successful land developer, at a flower show. Crow mentioned that he couldn't make a decent return on income. Stemmons suggested that Crow try constructing a building. This first building, a warehouse, was so successful that Crow built 300 more. Today these warehouses are worth about $100-million, and Crow owns 50 per cent of them. He has also branched out to apartment houses, trade marts, office buildings, etc. Currently he files federal income tax returns for 35 corporations, 75 partnerships, plus 20 separate trusts for his children. And it all started at a flower show!

SEEK WIDER SUCCESS WITH YOUR SKILLS

Many talented people work at only one job or one business. They earn a fair income but never hit the big money because they use only a tiny part of their skills. If they only had enough courage, and drive, to branch out and use more of their skills they might earn more and have more fun in life. Here are seven examples of highly successful and talented people who branched out.

Al Stahl is part owner of a busy electronics company. He also owns a successful delicatessen and has interests in real estate, life insurance, and a decorating store. Al began his business career as an engineer. Talking about himself and his busy teacher-wife, Al remarks, "We enjoy leisure but not as a full-time career. It's much more satisfying using your skills and abilities."

Albert Stockli, executive chef of Restaurant Associates, directed the kitchens of many luxury restaurants, including THE FOUR SEASONS, THE FORUM OF THE TWELVE CAESARS, *and the* TOWER SUITE. Recently he resigned to become co-owner of the *Stonehenge,* one of America's best-known country inns. Meanwhile, he continues as a consultant at Restaurant Associates.

John N. Wheeler has been "selling other men's brains" for

years. "Early in life," says Mr. Wheeler, "I decided that I could make a bigger profit by selling other men's brains than my own and so far I don't think I have ever found myself wrong." Mr. Wheeler owns a news syndicate which sells articles written by outstanding people in all fields. Some authors whose work he handled include President Truman, Ernest Hemingway, Ring Lardner, and others. A writer himself, Mr. Wheeler recently sold his syndicate and may open an advisory service to assist editors buying stories from syndicates.

Five women—Edna Raphael, Sue Haber, Ann Gertler, Kathy Zarrelli, and one other—are members of the Wall Street Technicians and Analysts Society, a select group once a men-only organization. Former housewives, secretaries, and clerks, these women are outstandingly successful today. Kathy Zarelli made her obstetrician $162,00 on his first buy.

Jerome Taishoff is in investments banking, electronics, synthetic mica, education, and a variety of other activities. Known throughout the world as a top-notch salesman, Mr. Taishoff developed a formula for producing synthetic mica for use in aerospace, aviation, electronics, and telemetering products. His many activities enable him to be an active philanthropist and patron of the arts during his frequent world-wide trips.

Joshua Cohen began work as an electric lamp assembler. In his spare time he used the facilities of the lamp factory to develop his own ideas because he believed in his inventive skills. He invented magnesium flash powder used by photographers to provide light. Another invention was a small toy train which ran on tracks. The trains were so popular, Mr. Cowen formed the Lionel Corporation to manufacture them. Today almost every boy knows of Lionel trains.

Mrs. Katie Lewin is a housewife and mother who enjoys jigsaw puzzles. A circular jigsaw puzzle Mrs. Lewin's husband brought home from England was such a big hit with the family and friends that Mrs. Lewin decided to go into the business of manufacturing and selling puzzles. Mrs. Lewin decided to use famous paintings on her puzzles. Today she has what is said to be the most difficult puzzle in the world— "Convergence". Salvatore Dali made one painting, *Double Image,* especially for use as a jigsaw puzzle.

Find New Ways to Use Your Skills

Seek out new ways to use your skills. Don't sit back and relax while you use only one skill. Get out and sell a second, or third skill.

If you have only one skill, learn a second and a third. Take a course in evening school or by correspondence. Increasing your skills will raise your earning power and improve your security in life. Try it and see for yourself.

Dream Yourself to New Skills

Think back on your past life. Did most of your dreams come true? Did you get the job you wanted, marry the girl or man you chose, or go to the school you wanted to attend? If you did, then you know you can make most of your dreams come true. If you didn't, then it's time you learned how to make your dreams come true.

When you imagine you have achieved the success you desire, you release many positive forces in your life. These positive forces increase your chances for success when you face real situations in life. Your dreams prepare you for success and you act like a professional, even though you may be using a new skill for the first time.

Six Steps to New Skills

Use your imagination to build success with new skills by taking these six steps:

(1) Choose the new skill you'd like to acquire
(2) Read as much as you can about this skill
(3) Obtain copies of the catalog of several colleges and universities giving courses in the skill; read the content of every course
(4) Observe, if possible, people using the skill; watch what they do; read the documents they produce
(5) Imagine yourself in school studying this skill. In your mind, hear the teacher; see him write on the blackboard; feel the knowledge pour into your mind.

(6) Observe yourself, in your mind, as you actually work on a job, using your newly acquired skill. Visualize the problems you'll meet and how you'll solve them. Imagine the compliments you'll receive from your boss.

When is the best time for you to dream your way to new skills? Only *you* can answer. But here are typical times that people find useful for imagining success in the skills they desire:

(a) In the evening, just after retiring
(b) While traveling by car, train, bus, plane
(c) During a walk, swim, game, or other sport
(d) While relaxing anywhere

Find Your Best Skill-Building Time

Find the best time for yourself by trying to imagine yourself using your new skills. Perhaps the best time of all is just after you retire in the evening. Images built at this time are usually more vivid and are retained by the mind longer. The success you imagine while you are relaxed seems to build a greater driving force you can put to work the next day. This may not be true for everyone and you may find another time is more effective for yourself.

Dream yourself to new skills and a quick fortune may be yours. Neglect dreams and you overlook one of the most potent forces at your command.

You have, or can develop, a gold-mine of skills. Exploit the secret wealth of these skills and you'll reach your wealth goals sooner and with fewer problems along the way. You'll quickly become a smart money wealth builder because you use this powerful shortcut which has been a closely held secret of many of the world's millionaires.

CHAPTER 8

Diversify to Millionize Your Income

*You can build a quick fortune
selling only one skill, being in
only one business, or handling only one product . . .*

In fact, many successful fast fortune builders will tell you that you need only *one* good idea to build a smart money fortune.

Both these statements are true for some people. I know many shortcut wealth builders who are striking it rich using the one-business technique. But in writing this book I am so interested in helping *you* get rich quickly that I want to show you every possible way. I want to make *you* one of the five hundred new millionaires who join this magic wealth level every year in the United States. Diversifying to millionize your income is a powerful way to build maximum income in the shortest time. Let's see why.

Diversifying Increases Your Chances for Success

Every business activity, whether you work for yourself or for someone else, is a risk situation. In a young, small business the risk of failure is high. On a new job, working for someone else, you have the risk of being fired if your boss doesn't like the work you do.

But suppose you have two businesses or two jobs. What then? You may fail in one business or job but you always have the other to turn to. With two or more activities your chances for success are much greater.

Almost every new millionaire who built his fortune in the last ten years has diverse business interests. True, many of these quick wealth builders start with only one activity and a bankroll of OPM (Chapter 6). But once they make a few dollars they quickly diversify their business interests. Thus, a man who starts a shipping line will soon own a shipyard, a row of apartment houses, a factory, etc. Within a year or two he has money coming from many different sources.

In my own business activities I have built a tidy personal fortune using the diversification principle. I work as a business executive in the publishing field; in my free time I write books such as the one you are now reading; I teach courses; I own three small businesses in two different fields; I consult, for a fee, on various business and engineering problems; I write, and actively sell, magazine articles; I invest, and make money, in the stock market. During my busy career I've made money in hotels, apartment houses, rental real estate, boating, shipping, publishing, product design, and several other activities. Having money coming from these many sources has, and is, keeping me in the things I want without worrying about what tomorrow will bring. So if you've failed up till now, try diversifying. You'll banish failure forever.

How Diversifying Will Help You

You have six advantages when you diversify your business interests. They are:

(1) Income from several sources
(2) Greater certainty of a steady income
(3) Easier financing of new ventures
(4) Opportunity to transfer funds among ventures
(5) Wider business experience for yourself
(6) Chance for greater achievements

No matter how or where you diversify, you stand to gain. Note that you can diversify on a job almost as easily as in a business of your own. You can use this technique in almost any situation. Many of the top corporate presidents I know reached their high-pay positions by diversifying—that is, taking on more and more responsibilities and diverse duties. Soon they became multi-talented —able to deal with any problem that might arise. Their diversity of skills lead to quick advancement and bigger earnings.

One surprising and highly beneficial aspect of diversifying which can't be measured but most certainly exists, is the greater confidence you'll gain. Having more than one source of income or skill reassures you, makes you more confident. You're more relaxed; you don't choke up. Thus, you do a better job, and obtain favorable results. This leads to greater confidence, more significant achievement—your success and fortune race ahead.

How You Can Diversify Your Interests

You can diversify in every area of profitable income. A friend of mine who holds a top executive job decided to diversify his income by investing in the stock market. Recently, after having invested successfully in aerospace stocks, he decided to diversify his stock holdings. His aerospace investments were so profitable he believed that the "satellite" aerospace companies, smaller companies turning out parts (motors, landing gear, electronic equipment, etc.) for aircraft and missiles, would also pay off. He was right. Today he is comfortably wealthy, all from stock investments.

Six Steps to Profitable Diversification

There are six steps in profitable diversification to millionize your income. These steps are:

1. *Decide how you want to diversify*—by taking another job in your off-hours, by buying a business and operating it by absentee management, by investing in real estate, securities, commodities, oil wells, or other ventures.

2. *Study the means you've chosen to diversify.* Does it have quick profit potential? Will you be reasonably happy working at this activity? Can you sell out quickly and easily if you want to or must? Is the price fair (one to three times the annual net income for a business)?

3. *Make dry runs of your plan.* See yourself working at this new activity. Imagine how you'll feel if you must miss important social events because you've taken on extra work. Review the costs, profit, and interest expense from every possible angle—don't stop until you're sure you've used every approach. Don't go ahead until you're positive you can "turn the corner" and earn a good income.

4. *Make your decision—then move ahead at full speed.* Don't waste time; push ahead as quickly as possible. You want to get rich fast. The only way to do so is by taking quick action, once you've made a decision. As a general guide in your search for wealth, take the advice of one of my rich friends who says, "Think slowly and carefully about every business deal; act swiftly and decisively once you make a decision."

5. *Regularly check the results you obtain.* Use an easily evaluated measure such as take-home pay, dollars of profit, etc. Check your results daily or weekly, depending on the income cycle. If your income begins to fall, find the cause immediately. Then take action to either increase the income or reduce costs while holding the income constant.

6. *Diversify your diversifications.* Don't be content with just one diversified interest unless you wish to restrict your activities and wealth. (Several men I know restricted their activities so they could retire in their early forties after building a reserve of $300,000 to $500,000 from their diversified interests.) Follow the same steps

outlined above for each new diversified interest. Feed part of the income from one activity to another. Always keep in mind the important principle you learned in Chapter 6—find a business or job which pays all its costs, plus an income to you, and you'll have a chance to build wealth at a fantasic rate—if you use your ingenuity and diversify.

Follow the Example of Successful People

There are thousands of new activities you can choose to diversify your interests. And if you're determined to use the magic million-dollar shortcuts to wealth you're learning here, you'll succeed at almost any new activity. For as Walter D. Scott, a well-known business adviser, said, "Success or failure in business is caused more by mental attitudes than by mental capacities." If you *really* want to succeed you will. Let's take a quick look at the diversified interests of some typical people.

Today in the United States 3,000 medical doctors own their own drug stores. Many of these doctors offer their patients a discount on the medicines purchased at the doctor-owned drug stores. Ophthalmologists (eye doctors) diversify their interests in a similar way—2,500 own their own optician's shops where eyeglasses are made and fitted.

In my own activities I diversified from mechanical engineering to magazine publishing to book publishing to recreational activities (boating and billiards) to business consulting. Meanwhile, my hobbies of article and book writing kept, and are keeping, me busy during the time I'm not diversifying. As Henry Ford remarked, "Business is never so healthy as when, like a chicken, it must do some scratching for what it gets."

From Lifeguard to Philantropist

George C. Semerjian is 39 and estimates his personal fortune as between $6-million and $10-million. Working as a lifeguard at a lake, he had plenty of time to think. He decided to buy an old boarding house on the lake and convert it to a restaurant to earn the money for his college tuition. Scratching around for money, he raised $1,000 and bought the boarding house with a new mortgage from a bank. The restaurant didn't earn as much as he thought it would so Semerjian diversified and began keeping the account books for Carl Martucci while going to college. Finishing college, Semerjian went into the concrete business and sold his restaurant. He hit it big in the concrete business because a major building boom was underway.

A few years later he sold the concrete-mix portion of his business and diversified into real-estate speculation. Today, after a number of highly lucrative industrial land deals, George Semerjian is a heavy contributor to charities. He is a leader in his religious group and enjoys helping retarded children.

Pants for Gals

Jack Winter opened a men's pants factory in a basement during a big depression. He struggled along for several years and then began making women's slacks too. Business improved. Soon, at the suggestion of his wife, he introduced tapered pants for women, because there were no styles on the market that fit women properly. Tapered pants were an instant hit and Jack Winter's company has grown rapidly. Today it is the leading producer of stylish stretch pants. Recent additions to his diversified line include swimwear, sportswear, junior sweaters, skirts, shirts, blouses, ski wear, yard goods, sewing supplies, etc. Total sales in a recent year were about $35-million.

Collector of Businesses and Art

Norton Simon diversifies by acquiring companies in trouble. He usually gets them out of trouble while increasing his own wealth. Though he declines to say how much money he has, his stock holdings in one company were recently worth $8.5 million. He has interests in many other companies and owns what is said to be the finest private art collection in the United States—Picasso, Van Dyck, Renoir, Cezanne, etc.

Mr. Simon began diversifying after he accumulated $35,000 from investments in the stock market and the steel supply business.

He bought out a bankrupt food company and soon had it showing a profit after reducing prices and introducing more efficient operating procedures.

Today Mr. Simon collects companies and art. He has numerous diversified interests in about 24 companies. These include firms in steel, meat processing and packing, soft drink beverages, broadcasting, movies, etc. His many interests keep him happily busy and extremely prosperous.

From Parking Lots to Motels

Two young men, Howard M. Metzenbaum and Alva T. Bonda, made frequent trips to the Cleveland airport to take short trips by plane. The field had little suitable parking space for cars. One day, while struggling through a sea of mud at the airport, they hit upon an idea. Why couldn't they pave, light, and fence this "cow-pasture" parking field, pay the airport for the privilege, and earn an income while increasing the popularity of air travel?

Their idea was almost an instantaneous success. During their first year, Metzenbaum and Bonda guaranteed $400 per month for the airport parking concession. Recently they paid the city of Cleveland more than $500,000 for the *same* concession.

Meanwhile, the two young men diversified. Today they operate downtown garages and parking lots in cities all over the United States. They have car-rental franchises in many cities, and operate airport motels and ground transportation facilities. Now these two successful young men are planning on using the air rights over their parking lots for motels. By expanding vertically they will have two businesses on the same plot of ground formerly occupied by one! This is an outstanding example of the creative skill you can develop as you diversify your interests.

Failure to Success

A man I know is an executive in one of the world's largest employment agencies. His present earnings exceed $50,000 per year. And as each year passes he earns more.

Yet two years ago this executive, Tom D., was in a rut which he says, "seemed forty feet deep. I thought I'd smother in it. My boss had taken a dislike for me and my work. He didn't fire me but he did stop salary raises. Then he demoted me, bringing in a younger man and giving him my job. I was miserable because I wanted to devote my entire career to this company."

"For three months I felt sorry for myself. Slowly I began to realize that what my boss had done to me was *his* decision. While it certainly affected my job, I need not let it ruin my life. I decided to study the job market to learn if I could find another, more pleasant spot."

"I read the employment ads in large newspapers for weeks. While reading these ads, important changes occurred in me. I became less tense because I learned that there were many good-paying jobs available. I could switch jobs easily. Also, I became deeply interested in the 'job business'—that is, the employment agency business."

"Soon I was reading books, reports, and articles about this wonderful business of helping people find better jobs. Since I knew many people in the accounting field, I decided to try to get a job with a firm specializing in placing accountants."

"I was amazed—during my first day of looking for work I received three fine offers of jobs. Several others were made later and I took the best. Within a few months I had a booming employment desk. I diversified my interests and found greater success. My ex-boss, incidently, still gets angry with people—but not with me because some day I may have to find him a new job!"

Later, in Chapter 11, you'll learn how other people profitably diversified their interests in their spare time without changing jobs. You can do the same if you wish. Meanwhile, let's see how you can finance your diversification.

How to Get the Money to Diversify

Your key to successful diversification to millionize your income is OPM—other people's money. Thousands of companies diversify by using OPM—why shouldn't you?

The key, as with other activities using OPM, is to earn enough income to (1) pay for the business, and (2) pay you an acceptable income for your efforts. Let's look at a typical example so you'll know what to expect when you diversify to millionize your income.

Payments You Must Make

In any business you start or buy you'll have five types of payments to make:

1. Fixed expenses—rent, light, heat, etc.
2. Equipment expenses—machinery, fixtures, etc.
3. Labor expenses
4. Mortgage expenses
5. Profit for yourself

Fixed expenses, item 1, are for the facilities and services you rent and use in producing an income. As a general guide *hold fixed expenses to the minimum level possible.*

Equipment expenses, item 2, may be included as part of a mortgage, item 4, or may be paid separately. Equipment payments are usually made monthly and run for periods of one year to five years. Thus the equipment payment becomes money-in-hand once you make the last payment—if the equipment has a useful life longer than the payment period, which it usually does.

Labor expenses, item 3, can be an enormous burden, particularly in the first few months of a business. Keep labor expenses low by doing as much as you can yourself, by hiring part-time help, or by employing members of your family.

Mortgage expenses, item 4, can be of several types. You may borrow from a bank to make a down payment on the business. You repay monthly; this is one type of mortgage expense. Or you may give the seller promissory notes for part payment for the business. You pay on these notes each month. Lastly, where you purchase property, machinery, equipment, or other assets, you will usually make a monthly payment. Mortgage expenses, which might also be called *note expenses,* eventually end and become money-in-hand. So the smart money shortcut fortune builder tries to pay off these expenses as quickly as possible, while holding the monthly payments to a reasonable amount.

Profit for yourself, is your reward for the time, effort, and energy you put into the business. Do not diversify unless you can see some potential profit in the business from the first day you take over. By following the plan in this book you will use your profits to build your fortune. But if you have some unexpected expenses in the future, as many businesses do, you can use part of your profit to pay these expenses. So never diversify unless you clearly see a profit opportunity. For as Charles Abbott, well-known industrialist, wisely noted, "Business without profit is not business any more than a pickle is candy."

Put Your Know-How to Work

You now know enough to be able to diversify into almost any business. Let's put your know-how to work on a recent business I investigated which the owners said had an annual income (gross) of $60,000.

The asking price for this retail marine-supply business was $60,000, with a down payment of $14,000. About $25,000 was owed on the equipment used in the business; the owners would take promissory notes for the balance, or $60,000 — (14,000 + 25,000) = $21,000, if I took over the payments on the equipment. I wanted to buy this business with borrowed money (OPM) because my credit rating is good and I want to keep it working on profitable deals.

Since a marine business of this type depends, to a large extent, on walk-in trade, I watched the place of business for several months. Business was brisk but not good enough to justify the one-and-one rule of thumb. This rule says you won't go wrong if you pay a total price of one year's gross earnings for a business. Thus, this business, which supposedly did $60,000 gross per year, would be a good buy, according to the one-for-one rule, at $60,000.

To verify the actual income I sent my accountant in to study the books of the business. This cost me $100 for a day's work and was worth $15,000. Here's why.

My accountant found that the business actually grossed $45,000 during the previous year. He learned this from a study of the books and the income-tax returns. He also found that there were a number of unpaid bills which must be cleared up before he'd allow me to buy the business. As part of his work, the accountant furnished me detailed income and expense statements for the business since its founding, three years prior to our investigation. These statements enabled me to check the income and expenses for each month and to compare them from one year to the next. This study showed me that the business was sick because it was poorly managed. I decided that, with some personal management, some good advertising, and adequate publicity, the business could be improved. My accountant agreed; I decided to make my offer.

How to Frame a Buy Offer

This was my offer: Total price $45,000 (using the one-for-one rule); cash $8,000; notes to the owners $12,000; the equipment notes of $25,000 would be taken over by myself. The owners hesitated for a week but then accepted my offer. I was delighted. Here's why:

Before making my offer I visited my banker and applied for a $14,000 loan for three years. He agreed to make the loan if I would show him the purchase contract. This is a routine request, to which I agreed. (He didn't want me going to the race track, a stockbroker, or some other place where I might foolishly risk his money). The $14,000 loan was a discounted type—I would receive $12,000 cash and would repay $390 per month for 36 months.

Now let's look at the monthly income and expenses of this business:

INCOME	EXPENSES	
$3,750	Equipment notes	$ 880
	Seller's notes	260
	Bank's notes	390
	Rent	1,200
	Light, heat	300
	Labor	400
	Total	$3,430

The difference, $3750 — 3430 = $320 per month, was my profit. Thus, I wasn't investing a cent of my own money, yet I had (12)($320) = $3,840 profit per year. At the end of twenty-eight months the equipment notes would be paid off and my net profit would jump to $3,840 + (12)($880) = $14,400 per year. And 36 months after taking over, the bank notes would be paid off, raising the profit to $14,400 + (12)($390) = $19,080 per year. Finally, after five years, profits would zoom to $19,080 + (12)($260) = $22,200 per year. Imagine this—$22,000 per year without investing a penny! Who could ask for a better deal?

Twelve Keys to Diversifying

This true case-history reveals twelve important steps to diversifying to millionize your income. These twelve keys are:

- Seek a profitable, going business
- Have an accountant verify the actual income
- Check the books and income-tax returns
- Use the one-for-one rule as a purchase-price guide
- Borrow all the money to finance the purchase
- Give the seller notes for the largest sum possible
- Obtain the longest note terms—36 to 60 months—possible
- Be certain the business shows a profit from the start
- Analyze potential profits with your accountant
- Always have a "cushion"—in this case labor—for emergencies
- Hire a lawyer to supervise the purchase
- Keep an eagle eye on all costs

Let's take a quick look at a few of the more important keys.

Buy a going business. Your chances for success in a going business are much greater because you can accurately check the actual income. Starting a new business from scratch is very risky because you are risking your credit rating and reputation on hoped-for income. When you buy a going business you know what you're getting, if you check it out carefully. Also, the equipment and fixtures cost you less because the owner never expects to recover his initial investment.

Hire an accountant. He'll earn his fee many times over and you'll learn much from him.

Inspect the books and income-tax returns. If these have been kept by a certified public accountant you can rely on them as being accurate and true. These records give the facts about a business; verbal claims are often inaccurate or exaggerated, as happened in the typical case above.

Borrow all the money to finance the purchase. Don't put any of your cash into the deal. In the above purchase the excess of the bank loan over the cash down payment, $12,000 − 8,000 = $4,000 was used to pay lawyer's and accountant's fees, tax bills, and other miscellaneous expenses. You work harder to repay borrowed money. This increases your chances of success. In business you want to have everything possible in your favor because you can't be sure of anything. Charles Eliot, a well-known business adviser, stated this neatly when he said, "All business proceeds on beliefs, or judgements of probabilities, and *not* on certainties."

Give the seller notes for the largest sum possible. This is very important. By having the seller take notes you reduce your cash investment and keep him involved and interested in the business. If the business isn't earning the money he says it is, he'll be unwilling to take notes because he knows you may go broke and he'll be left with an unprofitable deal on his hands. I've always insisted on notes in every deal. Where the seller was unwilling to take notes I declined to buy his business. Thus far, every deal has been a success—and much of this is traceable to insistence on notes to the seller. "Business," as Andre Maurois noted, "is a combination of war and sport."

Obtain the longest note terms possible. The longer the note terms, the smaller your monthly payments. The smaller your payments, the higher your monthly profits. True, your interest payments are greater. But interest is tax deductible—and easily proved, compared with certain other business expenses. So "rent" your mortgage money a little longer and live a little better while you can.

Insist on a profit from the start. Don't buy a business on the basis of *hoping* to earn a profit. Hope won't pay your bills or pay for the time you put in running the business. With a profit you can diversify into a second business, building a pyramid. In a recent year I used the pyramiding technique to increase my gross income

in ten months by an enormous amount, without investing a cent of
my own! If the two businesses in which I invested during that year
hadn't shown a profit, I'd be broke today.

Analyze potential profits with your accountant. A trained,
experienced accountant can give you many useful tips. You must
still make the business decisions but your accountant can clearly
recommend a yes or a no.

Always have a "cushion" for emergencies. Have a way to
cut costs in emergencies. In the above business I could have gone to
work in the evenings to cut the labor cost to $200 per month. Once
I made twelve payments on the bank notes I could apply for, and
probably obtain, an extension of the loan. This would cut costs
further. The same could be done on the equipment notes. Lastly, I
borrowed more cash than I needed so I'd have a few dollars left
after paying the initial expenses. Thus, I was surrounded by
"cushions". This is what we used to call a fail-safe system when I
was a mechanical engineer designing complex industrial plants.

Hire a lawyer to supervise the purchase. Don't skimp on
legal expenses. "Some of the biggest legal fees," says my competent
lawyer, Al Millus, "are paid by people who got into trouble because they didn't use a lawyer when they purchased a business.
People who have the proper legal advice pay nominal fees and
stay out of trouble." So use a lawyer—he will be a big help from
the legal standpoint, and may also give you some sound business
advice.

Keep an eagle eye on all costs. Know your costs before
you go into the business. Project your costs, and income, for the
next five years. Watch your actual costs every day of the year.
Compare the actual costs with your projections. If the costs become
excessive, take action to reduce them—use your "cushion" and
every other method available to you.

Diversify to Millionize

Xerox Corporation, one of the greatest successes in the
history of the world, saw its sales multiply ten times in six years.
Yet this great firm keeps pushing ahead to new products, new
methods. Joseph C. Wilson, Xerox president, has diversification on

his mind for two reasons: (1) diversifying helps keep the company growing rapidly, and (2) diversifying is a positive action against a too-narrow product line. "You can overdo it," he comments when talking about diversifying, "but if you don't diversify you can disappear."

You don't want to disappear—instead you want to millionize your income. Diversify and your chances of building a fortune are great. Sit back and wait for luck to come to you and you'll have a long, long wait. Get out of that rocking chair and do something different. Then just watch those dollars pour in!

You may even be as fortunate as D. Hillsdon Ryan and Donald W. Phillips, both of whom worked for big companies before they started a quick-service shoe repair counter in a department store. Today they've diversified to quick key-making, watch repair, appliance repair, plastic sealing, drape and shower-curtain production. In a recent year their gross sales approached $10-million. In a few years they aim to reach $30-million.

Get started on your diversification program *now!* You may become one of the 5,000 new millionaires listed on our tax rolls every ten years.

CHAPTER **9**

Find, and Market, the Unique, the Unusual

Today's world is one of
increasing sophistication . . .

People everywhere know more, earn more, and seek greater individuality in their homes, hobbies, clothes, and furnishings. No longer can the seller of mass-produced items expect to find a ready market for his products. People today seek something different from what the man next door has—and they are willing to pay for the difference. "Anybody can cut prices," remarked Alice Hubbard, "but it takes brains to make a better article."

Look Around You—See the Unique

Walk into a modern home or apartment anywhere. Look at the furnishings, decorations, and utensils. The chances are excellent that you'll see a chair or sofa from Sweden, an Oriental rug, a painting from Europe, leather goods from the West Indies, a radio, TV, or hi-fi from Japan, dishes from China, silverware from England, binoculars from Germany, lace from Ireland, and many other examples of the unique, the unusual. Each item is an expression of someone's desire to be different—to possess something which expresses his or her special interests.

Almost every new bride seeks a "conversation piece" for her livingroom; something that will get people talking because it is different.

As an amateur scuba diver I dive on wrecks of sunken ships, seeking a corroded bell, piece of crockery, or a running light to put in my study. Why? Because I, too, want to show how different I am. Such a "treasure" is certain to start a lively conversation about shipwrecks, sharks, and risking your life in deep waters.

Some men pay $10,000 to $25,000 for custom-built antique autos. Others collect rare coins or stamps. Women collect unusual buttons; others buy or make unusual flags, pennants, gowns or shoes. Everyday the world's prosperity increases. Men who were once delighted with black-and-white home movies now must have color film with a sound track. Complex $1,000, and up, hi-fi sets fill homes with soft music. People install enclosed, steam-heated swimming pools in their backyards. Others invest in rock gardens, lighted fish ponds, lawn sprinkling systems. Truly, this is a world of the unique, the unusual.

Young people, and not-so-young people, choose unusual careers. Thus, you hear of college boys and girls studying oceanography, celestial mechanics, orbital trajectories, and urban planning. Some unusual careers of ten years' ago, computer programming, data processing, and astronautical engineering, are now commonplace. More older people today are choosing "second careers;" the executive peace corps, management consulting, vacation counseling, introduction services, and hundreds of others. The world today is populated by dynamic, rushing, doing people who seek the new, the untried, the different.

You can cash in on this demand for the unique, the unusual, and earn a quick fortune—either in your own business or by working for someone else. All you need do is find, or create, a need and satisfy it. Let's see how.

Find the Need and Fill It

For years people have said to me, "Ty, if you're so smart that you can tell others how to get rich, why do you have to go on writing those books and articles? Why don't you use the methods you write about and get rich yourself? Then you can take it easy."

To which I reply, "I don't *have to* write these books and articles. But I *enjoy* writing them, and plan to go on writing until my last day. These books and articles encourage and stimulate people. I receive hundreds of letter each year from people thanking me for the help they've received from my various writings. These letters are as gratifying as the publishers' royalty checks. And as for using my own methods; I use them every day of the year. Today I *am* rich; tomorrow I'll be richer because I seek the unique, the unusual."

I was fortunate enough to sell my first article to a magazine for $5 at the age of sixteen. And, luckily, good fortune has stayed with me. Everything I've written since then has been published and paid for. Why? Because, the editors say, each article, each book, has a unique, unusual message. Editors were, and are, willing to buy, and publish, my "stuff" because they say it was and is different. It had, and has, an important message for their readers. I say this very humbly, recognizing that whatever talent I may have, no matter how small, was given me by a greater Being. Every night I thank Him for this gift and resolve to use this talent for the greatest good of the most people.

I firmly believe that everyone in this world—you, your children, your friends, your relatives,—was born with certain unique, latent talents. Each of us owes it to the world, to himself, and to his Maker, to make full, active use of these talents. And one excellent way to use these talents is by concentrating on the unique, the unusual—for the benefit of others. I also believe that so long as you help others, you will profit personally. Can anyone ask for a greater reward?

Profits in Picture Frames

Mario Broeders is a skilled picture-frame carver. He opened a one-man shop specializing in antique hand-carved picture frames. Mario thought he had found a need for unusual picture frames and that he could fill it. Two years after opening his "one-man" shop, Frames for Collectors, Mario had 26 employees and gross sales of $500,000. Mario is 34; in his third year in this unusual business he expects to have gross sales of $1-million.

Who buys hand-carved frames today? Many art collectors, museums, art dealers, and schools want antique frames for their valuable paintings. Mario uses specialized craftsmen to carve the beautiful frames; he pays his best men $250 per week. He trained all his employees in the intricate hand-carving process. To gild a frame with 22-carat gold leaf, Mario has his employees follow nine proven steps, beginning with the first coat and ending with burnishing with an agate stone. The secret of Mario's success? He found an unusual need and filled it with high-quality work.

Serving Skiers Builds Business

Marvin E. Burke has been a sportsman all his life. As a youth he played semi-pro baseball, basketball, and football. Another of his interests is skiing, which grew from his activity in the ski-wear market. Detecting a need for warm, strong, and stylish ski jackets, Burke introduced the quilted ski jacket. Based on a wartime development, the quilted ski jacket is lightweight, warm, and allows easy movement of the body. Business boomed as more people became interested in skiing. In a recent year his company, Sportcaster, Inc., sold $2-million in ski jackets.

To ensure continuing success for his products and to learn as much as possible about the skiing business, Marvin Burke bought a ski lodge. Here he tested his jackets, making certain that each was suitable for active skiers. He sold his ski lodge at a profit and now is president of a company which operates a ski resort. He is also president of Sportcaster, Inc., and a hockey team, the Seattle

Totems. The secret of his success? Finding an unusual need and filling it with carefully designed and fully researched and developed products of superior quality.

Ten Steps to Finding an Unusual Need

People throughout the world have unusual needs. Sometimes the need is obvious, such as a self-service laundry for a densely populated neighborhood where people can't afford their own washing machines. Or the need may not be too obvious, such as the desire of people to reproduce the page of a book in the library. Yet if you could fill both these needs you could become wealthy in a few years. Now let's see how you can systematically search for unusual needs.

1. *Look and listen.* Learn what people want.
2. *Read widely.* Many newspapers and magazines contain excellent ideas for you.
3. *Examine your own needs.* Is there anything you need that other people also would like to have?
4. *Ask people what they need.* Do some market research on your own.
5. *Think.* Try to find what people could, and would, use if it were available to them.
6. *Be alert* to new trends, new fads, new interests. Unusual needs are often revealed by new trends.
7. *Keep up to date.* Don't fall behind as the years pass. Modernize your knowledge so you're fully aware of what people want *today.*
8. *Make friends everywhere.* Look to your friends for helpful ideas about what they need, and why they need it.
9. *Be active in important groups*—business associations, clubs, political parties, etc. Circulate. Get to know as many people as possible.
10. *Travel—learn how other people live.* Broaden your outlook, your thinking, your alertness for unusual ideas and needs.

Note that each of these ten steps aims at getting you into activities that are important sources of unusual ideas. Thus, a good friend of mine balked when his wife agreed that the couple would become members of a local bridge group. Soon, however, he found that he enjoyed the stimulation of the bridge game and the conversation because his wife had chosen an intelligent group. One night he heard two women talking about antique telephones; both gals wanted to buy and install one of these phones. My friend knew of a batch of old-fashioned phones for sale. The next day he took an option on the phones and was soon installing them in many homes. Today he sells antique and special phones throughout the world. One set, made of jade, sells for $1,100. A recent ruling by the major phone companies, approving non-standard phones should make his business boom.

Put Your Ideas to Work

Once you discover an unusual need, do something about it. Make a study of the demand for the service or product. Find out how many people will buy what you offer. This is called *market research* by professors of business administration; the working businessman may not be so formal in naming what he does, but the steps he takes are the same.

Be careful to avoid overenthusiasm for your idea when you are doing market research. Your extreme enthusiasm may lead people to give you wrong answers, leading to errors in your estimate of the size of the market.

Read at least one good book on market research. Two which I've found useful are:

> Richard D. Crisp, *Marketing Research,* McGraw-Hill Book Company
> Walter J. Talley, Jr., *The Profitable Product,* Prentice-Hall, Inc.

Shortcuts to Profitable Market Research

I use, with great success, several shortcuts in my market research. Professional market researchers might snicker at these shortcuts but the methods work for me and they should work for you, if you want to try them. You might earn enough with these shortcuts to permit you to *hire* a market researcher some day. Here are the shortcuts.

1. *Talk to people in the business.* No matter how unique your product or service, someone is in a similar business. Spend several hours talking to three or more people in the business. But *listen* instead of talking. Make notes immediately after the interview, not during it. Some businessmen "freeze up," refusing to talk when they see you with a notebook and pencil in your hand.

It is my personal belief that you can learn much more much faster by talking to people in the business than by any other means. A businessman or someone working in the field can give you an excellent idea of the income, expenses, taxes, and problems. Getting this information from people actually working in the field you're considering will put you in touch with true facts.

2. *Visit several business places.* See the business, or job, at work. Notice the type of customer, type of employee, average amount of a sale, probable average pay, and probable income. See, hear, and learn what kind of equipment you'll need or use, how much it will cost, and the problems it will give you.

3. *Think of the numbers of this business.* Sit in a quiet spot at home with a pad of paper and a pencil in front of you. Estimate the "numbers" of this business or job, i.e. the total income, the total expenses, the profits. Use the information you gathered in Steps 1 and 2 as the basis for your estimates. Don't be afraid to guess at a number you are uncertain about. This technique, called *guesstimating,* is widely used by successful businessmen and executives everywhere. As you gain experience your guesses become more accurate, and you gain confidence.

4. *Check out your findings.* This is the most important shortcut of all. And I'm about to give you a secret technique that has never, so far as I know, appeared in print before. It is such a valuable way to golden riches that men have paid thousands of dollars to learn it. Others refuse to tell even their wives, for fear that the word will leak out. Here's this millionaire-maker shortcut: *Check your findings with a reputable business broker or employment manager.* These two people, the business broker and employment manager, know more about the business and labor situa-

tion in your area than anyone else. What's more, their advice is free, and unbiased.

Consult the Experts

When I'm thinking of buying a business I contact a local business broker. He can tell me (a) typical going prices for such a business, (b) take-home profit, (c) rent and labor costs, and (d) other expenses. The business broker has many valuable rules of thumb; for instance, in the billiard business, you shouldn't pay more than $50 per month per pool table in rent. Thus, the maximum rent for a room having ten pool tables would be ($50)(10) = $500 per month.

A good business broker can also help you find money to finance a business, particularly if he negotiates the purchase. One broker I deal with is active in business financing, acquisitions, mergers, real estate, and similar activities. He also publishes a worthwhile newsletter containing many business leads and ideas. This broker is a valuable adviser and friend. He also pays me a finder's fee on deals I find and he completes. You can work out a similar arrangement without investing a cent. Just ask any broker.

An employment manager can give you the straight facts on going wage rates for a given job in your area, facts on profit-sharing schemes, terms for employment contracts, and similar insider's information you couldn't obtain elsewhere. He can clear away the misinformation many people have about the true earnings for a given job.

Recently, on a business flight from San Francisco to New York, a young man in my firm passed a remark which clearly indicates how badly salary facts can be twisted. "I hear," he said, "that Charlie T. earns $55,000 per year." I nearly fell out of my seat onto Salt Lake City, thirty-five thousand feet below the smoothly purring jet.

"Where did you hear this?" I asked.

"Oh, all around," he replied.

"Charlie T.," I said, "is earning $17,000 per year—not $55,000. I know his exact salary because I just approved a raise of $500 a year for him."

The young man's eyes opened wide and I could sense the disappointment he felt. Because I spoke with authority, he believed me. And he saw that the income he might earn if he had Charlie T.'s job would be much less than he had previously imagined.

This is a typical example of how a lack of facts can mislead people about salaries. There is a common tendency to overestimate the salaries paid in various industries. Make friends with an employment manager if you want accurate facts.

Fourteen Unique Successes

You now have all the tools you need to find and market the unusual—be this a product or a unique skill you might develop in yourself. But before you begin seeking the unusual I'd like to have you see how fourteen others found and developed an unusual but useful service, product, or skill. By observing their methods and successes you will acquire useful ideas and techniques.

1. *New use for old bombers.* Millions of us use Flit guns every summer to rid our homes of summer bugs. Few of us think of the much bigger bug-killing job many farmers face. Hugh Wheelless does. He owns and uses, in his successful crop-dusting business, eight World War II bombers; two B-17s (the Flying Fortress) and six B-25s. With one B-17, Hugh's pilots can dust 875 acres, compared with 37.5 acres for a single-engine duster. Since ground time is lost time, the longer he can keep his planes at work in the air, the less Hugh must charge the farmer for the dusting. Thus, he switched to the big surplus bombers. Today one of his B-17s dusts 7,000 acres on one trip. In a recent year, Hugh's crop-dusting business grossed nearly half a million dollars and he expects it to grow bigger. Why? Because Hugh Wheelless is providing a low-cost solution to a common problem by using unusual means.

2. *Scenic backgrounds for rent.* Mrs. Robert Fleer locates and rents scenic backgrounds for various purposes. Her firm, Backgrounds Unlimited, which she founded, works with television commercial producers, advertising agencies, and photographers. She supplies a requested background; an old-fashioned dentist's office, a waterfront bar, a stable, private tennis courts, a Cape Cod house, etc. The photographers bring their models and snap the

pictures they want. Mrs. Fleer charges the producer, agency, or photographer a fee for use of the background and splits this fee with the owner of the property. Thus a few hours' harmless use of the property returns a fee to the owner and Mrs. Fleer, while providing an unusual background for the photographer. Many producers and photographers save themselves long trips and heavy expenses by using Mrs. Fleer's backgrounds. Her business is booming because she provides the unusual, the unique.

3. *He could earn $10,000 per week, if he had time.* "Killer Joe" Piro, whose given name is Frank, is the Jet Set's most popular dancing teacher. He started as a jitterbug and has been dancing ever since, teaching the mambo, cha-cha, merengue, twist, frug, frog, watusi, wobble, etc. Today he has his own dance studio and charges $25 per hour for dancing lessons. Two assistant instructors arrange the bookings for Joe. If he could teach everyone who wants lessons from him, he could earn $10,000 per week. Killer Joe Piro is an outstanding dance teacher because he keeps up to date and knows what his students want.

4. *She makes dogs obey.* Blanche Saunders teaches dogs to obey their masters. The obedience system she uses is so effective that a dog who successfully finishes her course receives a "degree" —starting with CDX (Companion Dog, Excellent) and ending with UDT (Utility Dog Tracker). Her obedience training is so popular that she has diversified (Chapter 8) so she can offer a complete service. She owns and operates Carillon Kennels, teaches, gives demonstrations, and writes books about dogs. Her famous book *Training You to Train Your Dog* has sold more than 100,000 copies. Blanche Saunders offers a unique service which many dog owners need and use.

5. *Antique tubes return high profits.* This is the day of the transistor, the solid-state circuit, and other advanced electronic devices. The day of the old-time electron tube is gone, so say some. Yet others, like Michel Levit of Levit's Metropolitan Supply Company, specialize in supplying antique, discontinued electronic tubes to a large number of buyers. Mr. Levit obtains his tubes in many ways; from government surplus, inventory close-outs, and from the tube manufacturers. In a recent year Mr. Levit sold $200,000 worth of scarce tubes. "Profits on hard-to-gets can vary between

20 and 400 per cent," Mr. Levit states. For instance, large, special-purpose tubes purchased at $7.50 each might sell for $50 each. Recently he sold several thousand computer tubes to a foreign air force. Purchase price paid by the air force was $1.80 per tube; cost of the tube to Levit, 5½ c each. Knowing what tubes may be in demand, and by whom, enables dealers like Mr. Levit to show a handsome profit on industrial obsolescence.

6. *Outstanding executive success.* When I sailed the seas as an engineering officer in the merchant marine we had an expression which quickly showed that each of us is different and approaches life in his own way. This expression, "Different ships, different long splices," often occurs to me when I hear of unique, unusual approaches to a common problem. It is much in my mind as I write about Meshulam Riklis.

Meshulam was born in Istanbul, Turkey, and came to the United States in 1947 with a wife, small daughter, and a little cash —$2,000 to $3,000. He spent the next several years attending college. One assignment was to study companies whose stock was selling at bargain prices. Meshulam enjoyed the study so much that "I became anxious to get into management, preferably by the control pattern, not the slower executive training route." After graduation, Meshulam became a part-time security analyst specializing in undervalued companies having a large book value. Soon he was organizing groups of people to invest in promising small companies he discovered during his analysis. Today Meshulam Riklis is Chairman of the Board of McCrory Corporation, which at the time of this writing is doing about $850-million a year in business. He hopes to reach $1-billion soon.

Meshulam Riklis combined hard work and accurate analysis to build a major business in a few years. He achieved executive success much faster than the man who joins a company and waits for a promotion. Thus, "different ships, different long splices." Meshulam Riklis used a different approach to executive success.

7. *Home for marked-down securities.* Many small corporations have a short life. Even a few large corporations decline as time passes. When a corporation fails or loses most of its business, its stock may become nearly worthless. This is where Percy J. Wien may take over. Through his firm, M. S. Wien & Co., Mr.

Wien bids on blocks of defunct securities. Prices can range from as little as one-half a cent per share to $10 per share. People are often willing to speculate on low-priced shares because revival of a company can provide handsome profits. As Mr. Wien observes, "Many penny stocks eventually become dollar stocks." Mr. Wien combines a creative approach to an unusual market and earns a profit by selling to brokers and financial institutions. And if he can't sell the stock to these groups, he can sell them for wallpaper in an executive's den or basement party room!

8. *Weekend antiques are profitable.* Arthur Brescani is a realtor; he's also part-owner of a hotel. For years he has collected antiques, particularly English and French items. Noting that his city, New York doesn't have a permanent antiques fair, Mr. Brescani decided to start one. He founded the Beekman Antiques Fair which is now running successfully on weekends. Dealers display their wares at the fair. The fair is running in Mr. Brescani's hotel, using unoccupied space. A nominal admission fee is charged; part of this is donated to a local school. Mr. Brescani is providing an essential and unusual service to antique collectors and dealers while aiding a school and a hotel. He's also enjoying himself because antiques are his hobby!

9. *Art that sells and sells.* Frank Lloyd, partner in Marlborough Fine Art, Ltd., and Director of the Marlborough-Gerson Gallery, is both an art connoisseur and a successful businessman. He summarizes his outlook when he says, "I want to help artists gain acceptance for their art, and I also want to make money, and lots of it." Said to be the world's largest commercial gallery, Mr. Lloyd's gallery features many unusual display techniques. Art prices are skyrocketing—$30,000 for a contemporary painting is not unusual, while a good Cezanne or Rembrandt can easily sell for more than $1-million. Frank Lloyd's business is booming because, as a former businessman, he speaks the language of his clients. "Art is a financial as well as a cultural investment," he says, "and I advise my clients with this in mind."

10. *Fast cars on a low budget.* Carroll Shelby raced sports cars on the world's famous tracks. He won the coveted LeMans 24-hour race in an Aston-Martin. Hanging up his racing goggles, Shelby turned to auto making; a tough business even when you

have a large amount of capital. Shelby started with hardly any capital and in its second year his company grossed $3.5-million and was headed for $7.5 million in its third year as this book is being written. Shelby's secret? He sells personalized high-performance autos. One of his cars, the *Cobra,* is built from an imported English chassis and body, and an American Ford V-8 engine with racing modifications of his own design. Now Shelby is modifying the Ford Mustang he buys from a local Ford production line. The modified car is called the *Shelby American GT 350* and carries its own nameplate. Typical modifications Shelby makes include a special four-barrel carburetor, a large size aluminum oil pan, hand-built twin exhausts tuned to permit top engine output, and many others. Today Shelby is appointing dealers to handle his fast-selling fast cars.

11. *Efficiency advice is widely sought.* Anne Shaw is one of the world's few women efficiency experts. She is recognized as one of the best in her field, and is so capable that she has her own management consulting firm. Recently Anne Shaw expanded her activities by forming a new firm which will advise companies on the use of computers. This is a booming field today because some computer manufacturers, and many computer users, don't know the full capability of their machines. A consultant, able to view both aspects of an installation, the machine and his client's needs, can often make valuable suggestions for better and steadier use of the machine. Among her other accomplishments, Anne Shaw writes books in her field of interest, directs management training courses, and is the mother of three children. She is truly an unusually capable woman who is outstandingly successful in a unique field.

12. *Riding the turnpike to riches.* Robert E. Petersen was only 21 years old when he was asked to publicize a hot-rod exposition. The sponsor withdrew before the exhibit was put on. Petersen and four associates had a choice to make: go ahead with the exhibit or get out. They went ahead and showed a $3,000 profit. Alert Robert Petersen noted that 42,000 young people were willing to pay money to see hot-rod cars. He decided to serve this market with a magazine. Teaming with an associate, he founded *Hot Rod,* then *Motor Trend.* Featuring many useful illustrations and bright, colorful covers, the magazines were instantly successful. Being young

and interested in young people, Petersen decided to branch out and founded *Teen, Power Boat, Karting, Skin Diver, Guns and Ammo,* and *Surfer.* As a skin and scuba diver and small-boat sailor who earns money from both these activities, I can certify that Robert Petersen's magazines are excellent; they are well edited and carefully printed. Now he is expanding again, becoming part owner of an auto racing track, and developing a skeet range and golf course. He's also in real estate, and now owns about $5-million worth. He's looking for more, because as Petersen says, "Real estate is nice to have."

13. *Ships and sugar spell wealth.* M. J. Ossorio was 21 when he went into his own business by operating freight ships between various Pacific islands. His shipping business prospered; seven years after beginning it he founded the North Negros Sugar Company. Three years later he founded the Victorias Company. All his firms grew steadily and Mr. Ossorio built a trade school near one of his sugar mills to teach young people useful skills. Thus, this highly successful businessman used his income to help others earn more, thereby increasing their income and happiness.

14. *Men help housewives do better work.* Two young men, Jean-Claude Girandot and a friend, started a mail-order service for housewives. Called the *Club of Good Ideas,* the service provides ten good household ideas to housewives every two weeks. Cost of the service is $3.20 per year. Within a short time after Jean started the club, he had 1,200 members. Jean expects to have 12,000 members at the end of his first year in business. He has plans for expanding his service to housewives throughout the world. What are some of the ideas he provides housewives? Here are a few: Removing tar from feet (use salad oil); put soap under your fingernails *before* starting a dirty job and you'll keep them clean; use wine vinegar, then alcohol to remove skin blemishes. These, and hundreds of other ideas, make life easier for the housewife subscribers to Jean's service.

Start a Golden Flow of Income

I *know* you can earn a big income with the unique, the unusual because I've done just this all my life. And I'm no smarter than you are; in fact you're probably much smarter than I am because you have enough sense to read a book on the subject. I tried to find books that would tell me how to earn a large income but I couldn't find them. So I went out and earned a large income. Now I write books in my spare time to help *you* earn more money in less time.

Take my word for it—I *do* want you to get rich. I want to see you on easy street as soon as possible. Find the unique, the unusual, and take it to market. You'll be richer than you think, sooner than you think.

CHAPTER 10

Go Where the Money is—and Make It Yours

Money doesn't have legs...

It won't come to you. So you must go where the money is, if you want to make it yours.

Six Successful Fortune Builders

As I started writing this chapter I thought of my many friends, and of the business people I know, who went where the money is and built quick fortunes. Here are a few.

Jack R. loves the sea, ships, and warm weather. So he moved to St. Thomas, V.I., and opened a boat chartering business to cater to the thousands of money-laden tourists. Today his business is booming. "I went where the money is," he remarked to me recently during a cruise on one of his boats.

Tom P. loves the snow, skiing and other winter sports. He couldn't afford to buy a ski lodge, so he went to work in one. He saved his money and was soon able to lease a ski lodge. His enthusiasm for the sport and love of the people in it brought him many customers. Today he owns the lodge. He allows me to use the beginners' slope whenever he needs some free business advice. Meanwhile, his bank account zooms.

Charlie K. is a successful flier. He operates an all-purpose airline in Central America. His planes, large and small, haul passengers, freight, animals, medicine, and thousands of other items. On a visit to his base, Charlie told me, "I'm here because there's money to be made. Good fliers are needed here." I understood what he meant when he allowed me to pilot one of his light planes on a routine flight over the hilly Central American land.

Alan J. sold his sports car to raise $3,000 to found an international research consulting firm. He believed that he could assist both European and American firms by helping them exchange technical and research ideas. Today his main office is in Geneva; he has branches in West Germany, Italy, France, and the U.S. Business is booming because Alan J. goes where the business is— on both sides of the Atlantic.

Bernard C. took a vacation trip to Europe. He saw immense business opportunities there and cancelled his return trip. Since he was a mutual-fund salesman in the U.S., Bernard C. decided to sell mutual funds in Europe. Operating from a Paris apartment, he soon had a booming business. In the first six months of a recent year his firm sold $300-million worth of mutual-fund shares in 118 countries. He expects his sales to continue to skyrocket as Europeans become wealthier.

John D. was a young tugboat captain in New York Harbor when he came across an old player piano. He took it home and reconditioned the ancient piano in his basement. Soon his curious neighbors were asking him to sell them one of the old-fashioned pianos. Today John D. is ashore. He "swallowed the anchor" as seamen say, and is the proud owner of a thriving piano business. While this is being written John D. has some 140 player pianos ready for sale. "You know one thing that brought it back?" John asks. "The rumpus room. You know, we had this togetherness in the old days. Then we lost it for a while."

Go Where the Money Is

"But where is it?" you ask. The money is in certain places. These places are:

(1) Where people live
(2) Where people play
(3) Where people use services
(4) Where people learn
(5) Where people seek advice
(6) Where people eat
(7) Where people work

The money is in the places where people are. People need housing, food, recreation, and many services; medical, dental, cleaning, auto maintenance, etc. As the population grows so do the needs of people. And as people become better educated and better informed they demand more from life. Almost everyone wants a bigger car, a more expensive home, better furniture, and the best tickets to the most popular plays in town.

A good friend of mine drove a small, low-cost imported car. He boasted that it was the greatest car made; nothing could rival its economy, comfort, driving ease. My friend got a new job (by following my advice) and within a month he had a shiny new fast gas-gulper of a car.

"Mike," I said, "I thought you loved those little imported autos. How come you bought this big gas gulper?"

"It has style," he said. "I'm earning big money now and I feel I'm entitled to a better car."

That's the story of almost everyone, everywhere in this world. Give a man or woman a taste of the better things in life and he wants more. This is why the money is where the people are.

People Change with the Times

Once a week for the last fourteen years I've had dinner in New York's Greenwich Village. I teach a three-hour evening class in a university located on the edge of the Village. These dinners are as interesting as the teaching because the Village shows you a slice of intellectual life in modern America.

During the middle fifties I watched, with fascination, the young Village beatniks and other free thinkers. Mostly young, the men often wore beards, dungarees, and black turtleneck shirts. The girls wore the same clothing. Instead of a beard they combed their hair in straight lines.

During these years I've watched the number of beatniks decline. One night I asked a beatnik why I saw fewer of his kind in the Village. "They're all getting rich," he said. "Most of them are buying houses on Long Island, in Westchester, or Connecticut. Once a guy and gal get a little dough, they give up protesting against society. Instead, they want to join it!"

So it goes. You can use your knowledge of the people in your area, hobby, or occupation to build a quick fortune. Let's see how.

Check Your Money Skills

Here's a handy checklist you can use to focus your attention on your valuable money-making skills and knowledge. Remember, you need not travel thousands of miles to be where the money is. Often it's just down the street, or across the road. But you must get out of the house, out of a rut, out of your shell and go after the money. Only then can you make it yours.

MY MONEY SKILLS CHECKLIST

MY HOME AREA

1. I live in a .... area. (city, country, suburban)
2. People in this area need ....
   to live better. (new housing, etc.)
3. People in this area need ....
   for recreation. (roller-skating rink, bowling alley, etc.)

4. People in this area need a .... store to service their needs. (clothing, stationery, etc.)
5. Other services people in this area need are .... (hospital, educational, etc.)
6. My past experience fits me to render .... service in my area.
7. The income I'd receive for providing this service would be about $............ per year.
8. I .... (could; could not) expand this business if I wanted to.

OTHER AREAS

9. People in other areas need .... (housing, recreation, etc.)
10. I .... (could; could not) satisfy these needs.
11. To satisfy these needs, I'd have to raise $................ in capital.
12. My chances of raising this capital are .... (good; poor).

Fill out this checklist now. You'll enjoy doing it and you'll learn more about yourself and your chances of becoming wealthy.

Where you can render a service to industries, firms, or other organizations, substitute their name for the word people in the checklist. Thus, many fortunes are built by serving industry. But since the number of firms is limited, your greatest chances usually are with people, as the following success story shows.

Two young Massachusetts brothers, Curtis Blake and S. Prestley Blake, couldn't find a job. So they decided to make their own jobs by opening a small soda fountain in Springfield, Mass. They borrowed $547 to open their first shop. Soon they opened a second shop. Today they have 107 shops in four states—Massachusetts, New Hampshire, Connecticut, and New Jersey. The Blake brothers plan to open 20 or more new shops each year. In a recent year their gross sales were $17-million. Imagine selling 2 million gallons of ice cream each year and four tons of hamburgers *per day!* This is certainly an excellent example of going to the people with an attractive product.

Today the Blake brothers have many plans for expanding their *Friendly Ice Cream Shops* to several other states. They're confident the business will continue to grow because not one of their shops has failed. Their profit incentive plan for managers, providing annual earnings in the $12,000 to $20,000 range, is one of the best in the industry.

Fill a Need at Moderate Cost

Reginald Miles Ansett started a one-man taxi business with a second-hand Studebaker he bought for $156. Today he does a $90-million-per-year business with some 70 companies. These include an airline, hotels, TV, and transportation. Beginning with a used auto didn't stand in Ansett's way. He recently completed the purchase of three new Boeing jets for $23-million. Mr. Ansett came a long way from that $156 used auto. How? By providing a needed service—transportation—at a modest price.

Emmet J. McCormack also earned a fortune in transportation. Starting as a messenger boy for $1 per week, McCormack soon increased his income by sculling a small boat about New York Harbor and selling marine supplies to ships. Within a few years he saved enough to open a coal company. He specialized in selling coal to ships in the harbor. A few months later, McCormack took his first step in transporting people. He salvaged a sunken ferryboat and received six years' free use of the boat as his fee. Using this boat he set up the Richmond-Brooklyn Ferry Company. It wasn't long before Mr. McCormack really went to sea; he and Albert V. Moore formed the company which is now known as Moore-McCormack Lines, Inc. Today the company operates high-speed passenger and freight vessels to many different parts of the world.

Notice how Mr. McCormack filled a need at a modest cost. His products were diverse; marine supplies, coal, local transportation, deep-sea transportation. Yet in each case he filled a need at a cost people could afford. Today his business continues to expand.

Ed Mirvish is a trend-bucker. His business motto is "I go against the trend". He got his start in a dress shop which extended credit to its customers when almost every other store operated on a cash-only basis. Ed switched to cash-and-carry when other stores discovered credit. Today Ed has a personal worth said to be $2.5-million. One big money-maker in his many holdings is *Honest Ed's*, a crowded, busy, intriguing general store which attracts five million satisfied customers a year. Some customers line up for three hours before the store's opening time—just so they can be first in line for the many valuable bargains Ed offers. He uses signs, a daily "door-crasher" sale (like 4 pounds of spaghetti for 11c), newspaper ads, singing commercials in the store and on the radio, auction money, etc. In a recent year the store sales were more than $15-million.

Today Ed Mirvish is expanding. He bought a theatre and restored it to better than original beauty and condition. Now he makes it easy for people to buy theatre tickets by using a credit card and phone-order system. While directing the theatre restoration, Ed was developing a row of houses behind *Honest Ed's* store into an artists' colony. These houses sell antiques, paintings, curios —even perfume.

Honest Ed Mirvish is an outstanding success because he fills a need. You can fill a need too, if you know what it is and approach it with the same ingenuity, vigor, and dedication Ed Mirvish displays.

Serve Special Needs—at a Profit

All my life I've admired women because much of my success is the result of women who helped me. I find women are often more capable than men; women will keep their promises; they will help you when you need it. When it comes to spelling and grammar I always rely on a woman. If you write one book a year, the way I do, while you hold a top executive job, run several businesses, swim, cruise, dive, tinker with engines, vacation in the Bahamas, ski in Vermont and the Alps, and do several hundred other things, spelling and grammar are secondary to the creative task of getting your ideas on paper. Women know, and remember, the rules of spelling and grammar better than any man born.

Among their many other skills, women, I observe, are adroit at detecting and serving the special needs of many people. That's why so many specialty shops, unusual services, and skilled tasks are headed up by women today. Men could, of course, perform the same tasks. But not as many men have the sensitivity and understanding that is required for efficient performance.

In my many business activities I deal with hundreds of women. I admire them immensely and recommend that all fortune

seekers, men and women, try some of the techniques of the successful women mentioned in this book. Their unique techniques for
filling special needs almost always work. If they do not, check to
see what you may have overlooked.

List the Special Needs You Observe

You, in the city or town where you live, have a unique
advantage. Why? Because you know, better than anyone else, what
special needs the people in your area have. I envy you because you
know more about your area than I could ever know. You can start
a business, get a job, or run a service easier than any outsider ever
could. You are really an insider, in your area.

Look around your city or town today, tomorrow, the next
day. Open your eyes wide. *See* the special needs people have.
Listen. Hear what they want. Then list these needs. *Write* them out.
Here's a typical list of the special needs of people in a moderate-
size California town. Use this list as a starter when studying your
town or city. You may even find a fortune-making idea in the list.
Several people have.

TWENTY-FOUR QUICK FORTUNE-BUILDING IDEAS

Does your town or city need a:

1. Museum	13. Art gallery
2. Swap center	14. Picture framer
3. Used book store	15. Restaurant
4. Special school	16. Hardware store
5. Antique store	17. Theatre for live plays
6. Hi-fi center	18. Jazz band
7. Foreign-car repair	19. Coin-collectors' store
8. Marina or marine supplies	20. Hobby store
9. Bowling alley	21. Miniature race track
10. Billiard room	22. Riding academy
11. Employment agency	23. Sporting-goods store
12. Business broker	24. Beauty parlor

You can make a big income using any of these ideas. For
example, on Long Island, where I live, there are 94 bowling alleys.
In a recent year these alleys grossed $20-million. This is an average
income of more than $200,000 per year per alley! Now you

know why most bowling alley owners drive Cadillacs and wear $300 suits.

Swap meets, where you come to trade your old and useless belongings for newer and more useful things, are popular in the far west. Most people buy things at these marts; particularly poor people. They can obtain furnishings at the very lowest cost—much lower than in stores.

Sam Comfort runs the Paramount, California, swap meet three days a week and nets $50,000 a year. "People still have that old horse-trading instinct; they like to wheel and deal," Sam said recently. "Folks are bored with just going into stores and buying things."

Ray Rollins, a foundry foreman, discovered a new career in swap meets. He enjoyed them so much he decided to quit his job and earn his living by selling, swapping, and finding useful articles for meets. Today he travels the world doing just this.

Start Today–Don't Waste Time

You have, within yourself, all the skills needed to build a fortune quickly. If you didn't have the interest in building a fortune in as short a time as possible, you'd be reading another book, perhaps the newest novel or detective story. But the fact that you're reading these words, here and now, sets you aside and makes you different from those who hunger after wealth but do nothing about it.

You've taken the first step. You're trying to unlock the secret of building a fortune—preferably in a hurry. You and your family want and need things now. The sooner you can buy that new furniture, new car, or new boat, the happier everyone will be. Don't be discouraged. Start today! Take these eight fortune-winning steps.

Eight Steps to a Fortune

1. *Decide what you want or need.* List all the things you need or want. Don't be bashful. If you want a $100,000 Chris-Craft yacht, list it. Find out what others close to you want or need. List these items and their prices.

2. *Convert your needs to dollars.* Add up the cost of all the things you need and want. Apply a safety factor of 25 per cent. Thus, if you need $300,000 to buy what you want, find your real needs as $(1.25)(300,000) = \$375,000$. You now know, perhaps for the first time in your life, how much money you need to feel wealthy. Many people who complain about being poor have never bothered to take this simple but informative step. Don't you be *that* lazy—*take this step now to learn what wealth would really give you.* Be rich in your mind and money will begin to come to you.

3. *Select a way to build quick wealth.* Earlier chapters in this book give you hundreds of ideas for fast accumulation of wealth. Later chapters give you more ideas. Pick the one idea which appeals most strongly to you. If you can't pick a single idea, choose several. List them in the order of their appeal.

4. *Earn your fortune—mentally.* You haven't yet invested a penny in the business or job that will earn you your fortune, other than the money you have paid for this book. And you won't have to invest another penny while you mentally earn your fortune, if you use the proven wealth-building method given here. To use this method, sit down in a quiet corner and mentally imagine you are buying the business or applying for the job that will earn your fortune. Review each step you'd take, the obstacles you might meet, the difficulties you would meet. Continue imagining each step until you mentally reach your wealth goal. Don't take any mental short-cuts; mentally review each step several times until you're sure you know exactly what you'd face and how you'd overcome it.

5. *Put your wealth plan on paper.* Write out the steps you must take to turn your dreams into quick wealth. One man I told to do this looked at me in amazement and laughed. "That's impossible to do," he said. "How do you know, if you haven't tried?" I asked him. "I'll show you," he said. Two weeks later he returned with his list—3,812 items. "It works," he said, showing me the list. "Now I know exactly what I have to do. This is the first time I've ever known exactly what's ahead of me."

6. *Review your list, step by step.* Go over your list, examining each step. Cross out unnecessary steps; add new ones you overlooked. Don't finish your review until you are sure that you know that each step is necessary and useful.

7. *Take the first, inexpensive steps.* Write for catalogs; obtain free information; consult with people who know the business. Don't spend large sums of money; confine yourself to pennies for stamps and letter paper. Go to the library and read the business books applying to your interests. If any of these books will have long-range use for you, buy them. Every cent you invest in good business and self-help books will pay off many times over.

8. *Move ahead, if you're sure.* Your list and studies will give you enough facts and figures to permit you to make a decision. If your decision is yes, go ahead at full speed. Build your enthusiasm. This will give you greater momentum to overcome the rough spots you are almost certain to meet.

Put Your Know-How to Work

Two friends of mine had a money problem. Their problem was very simple: *The money was where they weren't.* This situation, the separation of man and money, is common. You see it all over; so do I. It is the reason why people complain of not having enough money to buy what they need or want.

Let's see how these two men, Harry T. and Jack K., solved their money problem. Their methods are useful to everyone. You may, I hope, find useful ideas you can put to work in your life.

How to Raise Your Income $25,000 a Year

Harry T. was fifty when he was first hit with an urgent need for big money. Married in his thirties, Harry didn't have heavy educational expenses for his children until he became fifty. Harry worked in an office and earned a moderately good salary. But he was in debt on his house mortgage, his auto loan, and a personal loan. So his salary was spent long before he received it. In fact, Harry felt like a rubber ball bouncing between his job, his home, and his wife. Harry's wife has a sharp tongue and she is always ready to tell him how dumb he is and how many mistakes he has made.

When Harry T. came to me for advice he was an unhappy man. He lay awake many a night trying to figure a way out of his money problems. His eldest boy was about to enter college and Harry needed at least $3,000 cash for the first year's tuition, room, and board.

Harry and I talked for almost an hour about his situation. The more Harry talked, the more discouraged he became. I was beginning to feel a little morose myself until Harry made a remark which revived my hope. Harry said:

> **"The older you are the less time you have to get rich and enjoy your money. So if you want to get rich in a hurry you have to pick a simple way to earn big money with little or no training. An older man hasn't the time for long schooling or for years on the promotion ladder."**

"That's exactly it, Harry," I said. "But where do we go from here?"

"I don't know," Harry replied. "I know that I need money and need it quickly. But how can I earn a lot of money quickly and honestly?"

"Harry, there are just two ways to earn big money fast. In a business of your own or on a high-pay job."

"I'm not interested in a small business," Harry said. "I'd rather work and allow someone else to worry about the payroll."

"Harry, there are three ways to earn big money on a job— as president of a company, as a high corporate official (vice-president, comptroller, etc.), or as a salesman. The first two take years of training and years of waiting on the promotion ladder. Did you ever think of the third—of becoming a salesman?"

Harry's eyes widened. "No," he said. "But I've heard plenty of stories about the big money some salesmen earn. They say some salesmen earn one-hundred grand a year."

"And more," I said. "Salesmen even have a club, *The Million-Dollar Round Table,* for the big earners. Well, what say? Are you interested in selling?

Harry thought for a while. "Yes," he said, "I'm interested."

"Good. I'm glad you are. Too many people turn away from selling because they are afraid to knock on doors to make calls. Yet once you overcome this fear you can earn big money faster than in any other job I know. Now here's your plan of action to get yourself ready for a big-money selling job in one month."

Here is the plan of action I gave Harry. You can use it exactly as is, if you want to make big money, soon, in selling.

1. Read—and study—every word in these ten books:

> Frank Bettger, *How I Raised Myself From Failure to Success in Selling*, Prentice-Hall, Inc.
>
> Frank Bettger, *How I Multiplied My Income and Happiness in Selling*, Prentice-Hall, Inc.
>
> Percy H. Whiting, *The Five Great Problems of Salesmen and How To Solve Them*, McGraw-Hill Book Company
>
> Percy H. Whiting, *The Five Great Rules of Selling*, McGraw-Hill Book Company
>
> George N. Kahn, *The 36 Biggest Mistakes Salesmen Make and How To Correct Them*, Prentice-Hall, Inc.
>
> Auren Uris, *Mastery of People*, Prentice-Hall, Inc.
>
> Vincent F. Sullivan, *How to Sell Your Way Into the Big Money*, Prentice-Hall, Inc.
>
> Willie Gayle, *7 Seconds to Success in Selling*, Prentice-Hall, Inc.
>
> Hugh S. Bell, *The Salesman's Rainbow of Success*, Prentice-Hall, Inc.
>
> Jay Arnet, *How to Develop a $1,000,000 Sales Presentation*, Prentice-Hall, Inc.

2. Start your personal *Salesman's Notebook* by making notes about the important facts you learn from the above books. Write your thoughts and plans in this notebook.

3. Scan the Sales Help Wanted ads every day. Concentrate on the big city dailies and *The Wall Street Journal*. List in your notebook the firms offering the big jobs—$25,000 per year and up.

4. Practice the principles you learn from the ten books listed above. Use them everywhere; at work, at home, at play. Try to convince people they should do things that will benefit themselves but which they may be unwilling to do.

5. Apply for, and get, a selling job at an acceptable salary and commission as soon as you feel qualified. Once you have the job, work hard to sell more than anyone else in your group.

Harry followed this five-step plan. Within a month he applied for, and obtained, a selling job which paid him $6,000 more per year than he was earning on his old job. This increase alone was enough to pay for most of the college expenses Harry's kids would have each year.

I watched Harry. Would he be satisfied with the $6,000 increase? Some men lose most of their ambition as soon as they receive a big raise. But Harry didn't. Within a year he had increased his income by $15,000. When I ran into him in Paris a year later, he was earning $25,000 per year more. We had a very pleasant evening on the town—at Harry's expense.

Why do I recommend that mature men and women get into selling if they want to earn big money fast? There are seven reasons.

Training is short
Pay is high
Mature people are enthusiastic
Mature people appreciate money
Mature people impress customers
Mature people work harder
Mature people are dependable

All these reasons apply to you, whether you are mature or young. Try selling and see for yourself. Perhaps you can equal the record of Louis Fink.

Louis Fink quit a job paying $25,000 per year to become a life-insurance agent. In the next 42 years Mr. Fink sold over $50-million of insurance. Even at the age of 60 he kept writing huge insurance policies. From age 60 to 67 he wrote $18-million worth of insurance. And in each of his 74th, 75th, and 76th years he wrote over $1-million worth! At the age of 79 he wrote more than half a million in insurance.

Selling can make you comfortably rich at almost any age. If you start early, selling can make you unbelievably rich. You can salt away more money than many small-town banks have in their safes. And selling allows you more time to enjoy your riches while you're still vigorous, youthful, and full of zest for life.

How to Raise Your Income $90,000 a Year

Jack K. was completely different from Harry T. When I asked Jack, who had come to me wanting to learn how he could earn more money, if he wanted a better job, he almost exploded. "The devil with a better job," he growled. "What I want is a business of my own in which I can rake in the money."

So we talked, trying to find Jack's strongest money-making skills. We didn't make much progress until Jack casually mentioned that the first job he ever held was as a porter in a large apartment house.

"Did you like it?"

"Yes, now that I think of it, I did."

"And did you ever think of owning an apartment house that would pay you big income?"

"No; but I'd like to mull it over."

After some thought Jack decided he'd like owning one or more apartment houses. I questioned him carefully: Could he take tenant complaints without getting upset? Would a few vacancies worry him? Was he ready to own a building for three to five years? Could he find people to make repairs? Jack gave a yes answer to each question. This meant we were ready to move ahead.

I told Jack to look for buildings in four ways:

1. Contact real estate brokers
2. Study real estate ads in several papers
3. Explore his own area, looking for For Sale signs
4. Study real estate ads in magazines

Within a week Jack found the building he wanted. It was a 4-story walkup having 96 apartments and 12 stores. Annual income was $79,000; profit was $17,000; cash required was $20,000.

Jack fell in love with the $17,000 profit; he wanted that income more than anything else. There was just one catch—Jack had only $200. He needed $20,000. What could he do?

Jack's financial history wasn't good enough to allow him to borrow $20,000 from a bank. The largest loan Jack ever repaid was $2,800 for an auto. But to be sure, I had Jack apply at his bank for the $20,000 loan. He was turned down because the only collateral Jack would have was the apartment house. This would make the bank a second mortgage holder on the building and the bank didn't want this. The same was true for a $10,000 loan. Jack was ready to cry. "Let's analyze it before you begin to cry," I said. So we wrote down the numbers. Here they are.

Annual income:	$79,000
Annual expenses:	
1st mortgage amortization	$13,000
1st mortgage interest	17,000
2nd mortgage interest & amortization	6,000
Taxes	7,500
Sewer and water	1,000
Fuel oil	5,000
Labor	6,400
Insurance	1,300
Repairs	4,000
Electricity	800
Total expenses	$62,000

Net cash Profit = annual income − total expenses = $17,000
Gross Profit = net cash profit + amortization = $17,000
+ $15,000 = $32,000

Note here that Jack will receive $17,000 in net profit each year. Suppose Jack were willing to take a lower profit for a few years? He could use the difference to pay off a loan. Thus, if Jack borrowed about $4,600 from each of five banks, he would receive more than $20,000 in cash. His monthly loan repayments would be 5 ($130) = $650 per month for three years. Jack's yearly net profit would now be $17,000 − 12 (650) = $9,200.

Here are the steps I had Jack take to close this deal. The time each step took, in days, is given after the step.

1. Borrow $4,600 from Bank A (3 days)
2. Deposit cash received in bank B to establish credit (1 day)
3. Borrow $4,600 from bank B (3 days)
4. Deposit cash received in bank C to establish credit (1 day)
5. Borrow $4,600 from bank C (3 days)

6. Deposit cash received in bank D to establish credit (1 day)
7. Borrow $4,600 from bank D (3 days)
8. Deposit cash received in bank E to establish credit (1 day)
9. Borrow $4,600 from bank E (3 days)
10. Deposit cash received in bank F (1 day)
11. Meet with building owner and attorneys (1 day)
12. Have a contract drawn; make down payment (3 days)
13. Have title searched and approved (60 days)
14. Hold closing; take title (3 days)

Jack had his building in 87 days. He seemed very happy until I heard from him a few days later. "I want another building," he said. "In fact, I want ten of them so I can earn $92,000 per year."

Today, less than two years later, Jack has his ten buildings *and* his $92,000 income. And within a few years his income will jump to $170,000 per year, after he pays off his loans.

(If you wonder how Jack could buy ten buildings in less than two years, when each deal takes about ninety days, the key is this. As Jack became more confident, he negotiated for more than one building at a time. Also, the banks were willing to lend him larger sums as his property holdings increased.)

Go to the Cash—You'll Love It

You can become immensely rich, incredibly rich, magnificently rich—if you go where the cash is, and make it yours. But you *must* go where the money is; you *must* take a risk; and you *must* work hard.

Where is the money? I've shown you many examples in this chapter. Look around yourself today. *See* with money-conscious eyes. Build a drive to earn as much as you can as soon as you can.

You must take risks. The people in this world who won't take a business risk wind up in a mediocre job at a modest salary. You must take risks if you want to hit the big money. In my personal business activities, which are many, I take many big risks because, to date, they have paid off. Further, these risks make every business I go into a big adventure. Since I love adventure, business has become fun to me, particularly when the profits are rolling in.

But I wasn't always interested in taking risks. I had to acquire the taste for it. If you are this way, start by taking a small risk, then a larger one. Soon you'll be looking for profitable business risks wherever you go.

You must work hard. Just being where the money is won't make it yours. You must work hard if you expect to build wealth in a hurry. The hard work you do today puts a dollar in your pocket tomorrow. My personal credo on hard work, which has always paid off, is: *Accept additional work and challenges as they occur.* You will, if you truly want to, find time and energy to do the work. Your income will rise and you'll be on your way to getting richer than you think sooner than you thought possible.

CHAPTER 11

Make Your Spare Time Your Big Money Time

*Sometimes I think there
are as many ways to get
rich quickly . . . as . . .*

There are people who sincerely want to become wealthy. Why do I think this? Because every time I meet a wealthy man or woman I learn a new way to get rich—*their* way.

Consider the Spare-Time Way

My favorite way to get rich fast, which may or may not be your favorite way, is to work in my spare time. For instance, I'm writing this chapter while in a jet some thirty thousand feet above the Atlantic, headed for England. "Why," you ask, "don't you watch the in-flight movie? Or sleep? Or talk? Or drink? Or eat? After all, you're going to Europe. Live it up!"

Certainly, I'll do all those things, *after* I've written part, or all, of this chapter. "But," you say, "won't that spoil your trip?"

No. Writing this chapter while I'm on this business trip will make the entire journey more enjoyable. I enjoy writing; I want to make you enormously wealthy as soon as I can; my own spare-time activities are making me rich. So I write from true, proven experience. Because I know what I did, and what I am doing, I'm anxious to see *you* do as well or better. You're as smart, or smarter, than I am. There's no reason why you can't earn big money in your spare time while holding your regular job.

Five Advantages of Spare-Time Wealth

There are many advantages to seeking wealth in your spare time. Here are five of the most important.

1. *Continue your regular income* while you earn extra income. Why give up a reliable income to try a risky new source of income? Start your new venture in your spare time while you continue your regular income.

2. *Have a source of capital* from your regular job. The income you earn on your present job can help you finance your spare-time business.

3. *Build your idea sources.* With two activities to stimulate you, ideas will come faster and be more lucrative. With only one activity you're more likely to go stale.

4. *Vary your tempo.* Your daily job may be the very busy type. If so, you'll probably pick a quiet no-rush spare-time activity. The difference between the two will give your life more variety.

5. *Learn while you earn.* Picking a different activity for

your spare-time work helps you learn more. This increases your capabilities, making you better able to hit the big money.

Thousands of successful people started their lucrative activities in their basement, den, kitchen, or a run-down rented building. From such a humble start they expanded to a large and prosperous business which is rapidly making them wealthy. You can do the same if you apply the hints and procedures in this chapter.

How to Start Your Spare-Time Venture

By working in your spare time you can start your business whenever you want. You can start this very moment, if you wish. One of the features of a spare-time business which is very important to all of us is the way it teaches us the importance and value of a few minutes of time. Once you start your spare-time business you'll work at it every moment you can. And you'll earn money from these spare moments of work.

To start your spare-time business, take the following four steps. They will put you on the road to a fortune sooner than you think. These four steps work; they've worked for many others, and they'll work for you.

Four Steps to Spare-Time Wealth

1. *Pick a place to work.* You need a place of your own, away from family noise and other interruptions. Your working space needn't be large; a corner of the basement, garage, attic, or a room will do. The main idea is to have a place where you can work in your spare time.

2. *Get the equipment you need.* In almost every business you'll need a desk, paper, pencils, pen, postage stamps, postage scale, mailing envelopes, and a book for financial records. You'll find you have almost all these items now. If you don't, wait before you go out to buy anything. Try to make-do at the start. An old card table will make an excellent desk; a simple notebook is suitable for your accounts.

3. *Choose a time to work.* I work in the evenings, usually

from 8 to 9:30 P.M. I also work on the commuter train I ride for an hour in the morning. If I can work at any other times while on a trip, or waiting for someone, I do so. But a major element in my proven and highly successful money-making activities is that I have a time, place, and equipment for spare-time work. You should have the same.

4. *Pick your spare-time business.* Use the techniques you learned in earlier chapters of this book. In general, the principles which apply to a full-time business are also true for spare-time activities. But to be certain you find a lucrative spare-time business that will make you wealthy in a hurry, typical characteristics to look for are listed below.

Look for These Features in a Spare-Time Business

Many wealthy spare-time fortune builders can quickly analyze a business opportunity because they know what features to look for. You too can develop your analytical abilities, if you know which features are important in a spare-time business. Here they are.

1. *Simplicity*—the business, and products or services should be simple, free from complex negotiations, contracts, and manufacturing.

2. *Low capital*—the business *must not* require a large investment of capital. For most spare-time business activities, do not invest more than $2,000 at the start.

3. *Easy production*—avoid, where possible, complex products requiring expensive manufacturing machinery. The simpler your product, the better it is for spare-time wealth building.

4. *Few hours*—stay away from activities requiring large numbers of hours to produce a return. You want to earn the largest dollar-per-hour return you can. So look for activities that bring you a fast return.

5. *Small labor force*—choose a product or service you can work on alone; one which requires a minimum labor force. Labor costs money and requires supervision time.

6. *Little inventory*—avoid a business where you must

maintain a warehouse full of expensive inventory. This ties up your capital and can lead to big expenses and low profits.

7. *Quick turnover*—try to find a product that will sell fast. The faster you sell the better your chances for getting rich quickly.

8. *Miniature lightweight products*—these make for easy shipment, lower shipping costs, convenient storage.

9. *Large demand*—it's easier to sell something that almost everyone can use. But if you can't develop such a product or service, try a specialized need.

10. *Specialized need*—you can make big money with a product or service having a clearly defined audience you can easily reach.

Avoid Problems in Your Spare-Time Business

There are certain activities, products, and services that usually cause headaches in a spare-time business. Avoid them if you can. Here's a list of the problems you should consider avoiding. Stay away from:

1. Food products designed to improve health
2. Medicines for internal consumption
3. Short-lived products (flowers, foods, etc.)
4. Sensitive products requiring refrigeration or heat
5. Items requiring extensive instruction before use
6. Delicate products needing extra care in handling
7. Explosives, fireworks, poisons, etc.
8. Services involving medical or legal advice (unless you are licensed)
9. Charities that spend more than they give
10. Wild claims of astounding results of any kind

Analyze your prospective part-time business for these and similar problems *before* you put any money down. Get started with a simple product or service which is free of problems and your chances for outstanding success are much greater. Take my advice and guidance; you'll earn more sooner, and with fewer headaches.

What About a Spare-Time Job?

There are hundreds of spare-time jobs available today. Nearly 20 per cent of our population is moonlighting; i.e. holding a spare-time job, or running a spare-time business.

I've watched thousands of men and women earn money in their spare time. My private conclusion is that the only ones who hit it big are the people who have their own businesses. People who hold spare-time jobs are at a disadvantage because:

    a. The pay is low or only modest
    b. They can work only 20 to 40 hours per week
    c. Fatigue soon sets in, reducing efficiency
    d. Spare-time jobs are seldom stimulating
    e. Taxes reduce the take-home pay
    f. There's little permanent future for you

The only time I ever recommend that you take a spare-time job is when you don't have the capital to start a spare-time business. If you take a spare-time job for a year or so with the intention of saving money to invest in your own business, you are making a wise move. You'll learn while you earn. And you'll be better able to run your spare-time business when you have the needed capital.

I want you to become fabulously rich. You can't pile up riches working for someone else, unless you have the rare luck of inheriting a relative's business. So look for your own spare-time business. When you find it, use the smart money magic million-dollar shortcuts you're learning in this book.

Twenty-Five Wealth-Building Spare-Time Businesses

Here are twenty-five spare-time wealth-building ideas I chose from my file of more than ten thousand ways to earn money at odd moments. Read these carefully. There's a good chance you may find many profitable ideas you can put to work immediately. Most of these activities require hardly any capital.

    1. *Newsletters can be highly profitable.* Pick a specialized

group as the target for your newsletter. Thus, you might prepare and sell a newsletter to dentists, machinists, truck drivers, stationery-store owners, disc jockeys, etc. The usual newsletter is four single-spaced typed pages, 8½ x 11-in., mailed weekly, twice monthly, or monthly. Subscription fees range from $12 to $100 or more per year, depending on frequency of issue, field served, and size of each issue. You can break even with about 100 subscribers to the usual newsletter. After that you're in the land of profits.

2. *Prepare resumes.* Each year millions of people change jobs. Most need resumes to describe their experience and skills to prospective employers. Yet most job hunters are not skillful resume writers. To get into this business, study several books on resume writing. Then take small two-line ads in the employment section of your local papers. As the business grows you can branch out into resume printing.

3. *Find scarce books for people.* Contact several large used-book dealers. Tell them you're going into the book-finding business. Get a list of their prices, terms, delivery schedules. Place two-line ads in magazines and newspapers for your book-finding service.

4. *Sell special products by mail order.* The greatest potential for mail-order beginners is in specialty products for clearly defined buyers like tropical-fish hobbyists, hunters, salesmen, etc. Why? Because lists of such people are readily available; the hobbyist or worker will buy a product that will help him; most specialty items are easier to sell than mass-consumption products. Read several good books on mail order before investing any money.

5. *Laminate unusual objects.* A friend of mine laminates obituaries for the families of deceased persons. He obtains the obituaries from newspapers and magazines. This may seem to be a morbid activity but his business is booming. You can also laminate promotion announcements, engagement and wedding stories, advertisements, diplomas, etc. The profit margins are high.

6. *Collect and sell art.* Art is one of the best investments you can make today. Almost every smart money wealth builder who likes paintings, sculpture, or other objects of art, eventually invests in one or more of his favorites. Some wealth builders

specialize in finding rare paintings. Edward George Spencer-Churchill paid $440 for a Verendell painting which was later sold for $41,000. A nightclub pianist, Leonid Hotinov, paid $7 for a portrait he liked. During cleaning the painting was verified as being an authentic Franz Hals self-portrait. About two years after being purchased for $7, the painting was sold for $205,800! This is an appreciation of nearly 3-million per cent in less than three years! To get started in art collecting, study several books on the subject. An excellent all-around guide is Richard Rush's *Art As Investment,* Prentice-Hall, Inc., Englewood Cliffs, N. J.

7. *Sell jokes, if you have a good sense of humor.* Disc jockeys, comedians, and entertainers will pay you money for original or unique gags you prepare for them. Since you can prepare the jokes at your leisure in your home, this is an ideal spare-time business. Handle all contacts and joke submission by mail. Consult *Writer's Digest* and *Variety* magazines for leads on joke needs and writing techniques. With a string of clients for your jokes, you can earn a good income in your spare time.

8. *Sell used books to students, book buyers, companies, libraries, and collectors.* Several friends of mine specialize in different kinds of used books. All do well. One likes used paperbacks; another specializes in books published in Europe; a third specializes in old comic books. Another friend, Bertrand Smith, Jr., was a railway mail clerk. He read widely. This reading lead him to the thought that people in his home town needed a good bookstore. He opened the Travelers' Book Shop near a railroad station. He soon had half a million used, out-of-print, and new books in his shop. This large number led him to change the name of his shop to Acres of Books. Now he has two enormously stocked and wonderfully successful book shops.

9. *Remail letters and packages from various cities.* Some people and businesses want their letters postmarked from a city or town different from where they live. You can charge 50¢ for each first-class letter you remail. Thus, your profit is 45¢ for each letter you drop into the mail box. Charge 60¢ per letter for domestic air mail. Rates for packages depend on the mailing cost and time required. Get a string of remailers in key cities around the world and you'll have an important service to offer people. Advertise your service with a two-line classified ad in various magazines and news-

papers. That's your only cost, other than postage and shoe leather.

10. *Write for trade journals.* I've made a bundle of money this way and have helped many others do the same. Get a copy of my book *Successful Technical Writing*, McGraw-Hill Book Company, for many useful professional tips on earning big money writing for trade journals. Janet Geister, a nurse, is so successful writing for nursing magazines that she gave up private-duty work to become editor of a nursing journal. Then she "retired" a second time, and now concentrates on writing for many nursing magazines. You can write trade-journal articles on almost any subject from accounting to zoology. Follow the hints in my book or in other books available in your library. If you wish, you can take a course in trade-journal magazine writing. Refer to *Writer's Digest* magazine for a listing of the courses available to you.

11. *Perform research for pay.* Use fact sources in your home or local library. Specialize in areas that interest you, or work on any subject your client requires. But approach your spare-time work with skill. Get several books on research from your local library and research the art of research. Then you'll know what you're doing when you take on your first research assignment. Find clients by advertising in writers', historical, hobby, and similar magazines. When doing research for pay, remember that you must keep your clients' needs secret at all times.

12. *Collect, and sell, scrap metal.* The biggest boat in my favorite marina is a $200,000 beauty. Every time I admired this boat I wondered what the owner did for a living. One evening he invited me aboard for a friendly drink, as boat owners are wont to do. I soon learned he's a spare-time scrap-metal dealer. Since then I've met many other scrap-metal dealers. Every one is wealthy, prosperous, happy. You can begin by collecting scrap in your neighborhood, using a car or truck. Learn how to identify the metals (lead, zinc, brass, bronze, iron, steel, etc.) you'll collect. Borrow a book on metal identification from your library and you'll learn quickly how to spot the various metals. You may find metal collecting so profitable that you'll do what some of my friends do. Using scuba diving outfits costing about $200, they dive on sunken ships and salvage valuable metal cargoes and vessel parts. One good friend of mine had a wonderfully profitable summer diving

on a sunken submarine and salvaging its lead battery plates which he sold for scrap.

13. *Draw cartoons for profit in your home, if you prefer indoor work and enjoy drawing.* Magazines, newspapers, and journals pay $5 to $100 per cartoon, depending on their rate policy and your reputation as a cartoonist. Some cartoonists turn out four finished pieces per hour! Even at $5 per cartoon your spare-time income can be good. When you get to the $100 class, your spare-time income can be big enough to allow you to retire forever. You can learn cartooning by studying several good books, taking a correspondence course, or attending school. And, like any other business, you can make big money by specializing. One friend of mine does only industrial cartoons. Yet he sells to hundreds of industrial magazines and has editors waiting for him to send them cartoons. His bank book is one of the biggest I've ever seen, yet this is only spare-time work!

14. *Sell used courses by mail.* Most good correspondence courses cost $100 or more. Often this is more than ambitious people can afford to pay. Yet they'd be glad to pay $20 to $30 for a used course. You can begin selling used courses by visiting or writing bookstores, auctions, and house-furnishings sales where old correspondence courses may be offered. Few people visiting these places are interested in buying old courses. You can also take a two-line ad in magazines and newspapers. Word the ad like this:

> USED CORRESPONDENCE COURSES WANTED. Top prices paid. A. Jones, Box 25, Hometown, Ind.

Sell your courses with this two-line ad in general circulation and men's magazines:

> USED CORRESPONDENCE COURSES for sale. Send for list. A. Jones, Box 25, Hometown, Ind.

You can also use a combination sell-buy ad thus:

> USED CORRESPONDENCE COURSES SOLD, BOUGHT. All subjects. Send for list, or send yours. A. Jones, Box 25, Hometown, Ind.

Sometimes a combination ad generates more sales than the single ad. The only way to learn is to try. You can earn a good income selling used courses once you build a reserve of them and develop ads that make sales.

15. *Be a rental agent in your spare time.* You can serve as as a rental agent for almost anything—apartments, autos, trucks, power tools, electric generators, etc. As an agent you own nothing, other than a few business cards. Your capital investment is nil. You act as the middleman between the person owning the facility or equipment being rented and the person renting it. Your income is the commssion you receive on each rental. The best place to operate a rental business is in an area having a large population. With more people needing your services, your income will be larger. Advertise your services in the classified columns of local papers and the telephone book.

16. *Prepare publicity in your area.* Be a part-time publicity man or woman. Many small businesses need public-relations help. You can prepare news releases for them, arrange press parties, conduct interviews, and provide other valuable services. If you don't know anything about public relations, take a good course in it. A good friend of mine started public-relations work in his spare time. He specialized in aircraft and aerospace companies because he was interested in this work. His business grew so fast that he quit his regular job. Today he earns $100,000 per year and works only four days a week. He has only four clients; each pays him $25,000 per year; he works 50 days per year for this fee. Thus, his daily income is $500 per day per client. "When I'm real busy," he says, I work five days a week. But that isn't very often! I like my golf game."

17. *Operate a duplicating service.* This is the day of the copying machine. Almost everyone, from child to grandparent, local businesses to industrial giants, want documents, letters, and other papers duplicated. You can make big money running a duplicating service in your basement, garage, attic, or recreation room. Some of the best machines cost only a few dollars a month to rent. There's another charge, usually 1¢ to 5¢ per page, that you must also pay. You charge the customer 15¢ to 25¢ per page duplicated, depending on the number of copies made, going rates in your area, and the regularity of the customer's use of your services. Hire a housewife to answer the phone for you during the day, take orders, and deliver copies of the duplicated materials. You can easily earn $5,000 a year to start. With smart promotion and advertising you can quickly build this to $25,000 a year.

18. *Start a service business in your local area.* Do you have a corner on some specialized knowledge, such as how to handle the passengers and freight flown by non-scheduled airlines? Or how to help several companies at once? Lee Stevens, a former artists' and photographers' model, knows psychology (she studied it in college for two years) and how to fly. She tried to get a pilot's job but the companies refused. So she turned to selling charter flights for the non-scheduled airlines. Today she runs Stevens Airlines Service, Inc., which has 15 non-scheduled airlines as clients. In a recent year her firm cared for 59,000 passengers and many tons of cargo. Attractive Lee Stevens even renovated JFK International Airport's General Aviation Terminal. Which service business is for you? Consider these: advice on money problems; collecting overdue bills for firms; keeping accounting records, etc. Everyone, everywhere in the world, needs more services. Provide these and you have a great future ahead of you.

19. *Collect, and market, valuable coins.* There's money and fun in coin collecting. If you bought $20 worth of Canadian uncirculated cents in each of the years 1954 through 1962, you would have invested $180. In 1965 these coins, according to coin experts, were worth about $14,600. This is an appreciation of 8,111 per cent, or over 900 per cent per year! Now do you see why coin collecting can be so profitable? Start your coin collecting right by studying several good books on the subject. Then go out and buy. You can hardly make a serious mistake if you buy from reputable dealers. Incidently, just to make your mouth water, if you invested $1,000 each year from 1954 through 1962 in Canadian uncirculated cents, the value of your $9,000 investment would be $731,500 in 1965! Isn't that getting rich in a hurry (you could sell your coins during any intermediate year for a lower, but still handsome profit).

20. *Prepare greeting-card verses.* If you've watched greeting cards in the last few years you know they are way out. The days of the sentimental verse that rhymes, line for line, are no longer entirely with us. Today many people go for the insulting card, the double-meaning card, the "modern" card. All these new trends mean that more, and better, greeting-card writers are needed. If you're new to this field, take a course in greeting-card writing. You'll find that it pays, over and over. The professional

approach will bring you more sales, sooner. See *Writer's Digest*, *The Writer*, and similar magazines for course listings.

21. *Collect, and sell, famous autographs, in your spare time.* A friend of mine supported himself by buying and selling famous autographs. He never missed a meal, but there were a few days when he ate hamburger instead of steak. Today he operates a flourishing live-wire autograph business in his spare time. Write to famous people, complimenting them on something they've done recently which you've enjoyed, or with which you agree. Be sure your compliment is genuine. You will often receive a personal thank-you note signed by the famous person. Search out book-shops, remainder stores, and estate sales. You may come across famous autographs in any of these places. Also, you can buy auto-graphs from dealers and resell at a profit.

22. *Run a correspondence club for lonely people, hobby-ists, writers, travelers, students, etc.* Millions of people in this world are lonely; they crave companionship, new experiences, friends, small talk. Some can't find an outlet for these desires in their local area. So they use the mails. Your best bet as a start is a specialized correspondence club—say one for people interested in entering, and winning, contests. Advertise in contest magazines using the two-line ad technique. Your income comes from the fees you charge people to join your club and obtain the names of others who want to correspond. Profits are high; the entire transaction can be conducted by mail. This is an excellent way to earn spare-time money. With several clubs going for you, the money will really pour in.

23. *Consult for a fee.* There are hundreds of business topics on which you can consult for a good fee. Do you know something about ship operation? Set yourself up as a consultant and sell your services to steamship companies. You can find a market for almost any specialized area of knowledge in business, engineering, science, human relations, etc. Finding your first client may take time. Be patient. Once you find that first one, others will follow. All you need to start is a business card, telephone number, and some good publicity. Writing trade-journal articles in the field of your specialty, item No. 10 above, may provide the best pub-licity you can obtain.

24. *Analyze handwriting at home.* All of us are interested

in ourselves, in the type of person we are, and the characteristics we have. Handwriting analysis is a proven way of learning more about ourselves. Study handwriting analysis in several books, by correspondence, or by attending classes. Then market your analysis skills in person, or by mail. Expand your activities by running two-line ads in magazines and newspapers.

25. *Arrange tours for groups and collect commissions and free trips.* Hundreds of groups travel overseas and around the country every year. You can collect big commissions on every tour group you organize. If you want to, and have the time, you can travel on the tour free of charge. To organize a tour, check the people at work, in your religious group, PTA, Boy Scouts, etc. You can usually arrange group tours in any area or organization where people want to travel. This is almost everywhere.

Twenty-Five More Money Ideas

I'm determined to make you rich, if at all possible. There are now about 90,000 millionaires in the United States. I want to make you the next member of this elite group. Studies of the 500 new millionaires who enter this group every year show that almost all earned their money from a business of their own. Few of these new millionaires inherited their money. And there are almost as many new women millionaires as there are men.

Here are twenty-five more ideas for quick wealth building in your spare time. A code following each suggestion quickly outlines whether you need special skills, a course of study, large capital, etc. Here's the code and ideas list.

MONEY-MAKING IDEA CODE

N = you need special skills
S = study or course recommended
M = minimum capital is needed
E = either men or women can earn money
A = advertise your services

25 MONEY-MAKING IDEAS

1. Run a gift shop at night	(MEA)
2. Collect and sell recipes for cooking	(SMEA)
3. Be a magazine correspondent ("stringer")	(NSME)

4. Take and sell photographs in your area (NSMEA)
5. Teach courses in your town (NSMEA)
6. Frame pictures for people (SMEA)
7. Run a repair service for home appliances (NSMA)
8. Operate an employment agency for domestic help (MEA)
9. Train pets for people (SMEA)
10. Write TV scripts (NSME)
11. Collect and sell stamps (SMEA)
12. Write a magazine or newspaper column (NSME)
13. Write speeches for pay (NSMEA)
14. Sell magazine subscriptions (ME)
15. Raise and sell birds or tropical fish (SMEA)
16. Write and sell short news items for radio (NSMEA)
17. Illustrate books for publishers (NSMEA)
18. Run a typing service for businesses (MEA)
19. Write and sell popular songs (NSMEA)
20. Design and sell bookplates (NSMEA)
21. Write and sell poetry (NSME)
22. Do ghost- or rewriting for businesses (NSMEA)
23. Run a hobby shop (SMEA)
24. Clean tavern beer pipes (SMA)
25. Operate a reducing salon (SMEA)

Your Spare Time Can Be Your Big Money Time

All you need is one salable activity to pursue in your spare time and you can become comfortably rich. For instance, editors and publishers pay authors more than $100-million a year for the words they write at home. As an author you can make part of that enormous sum yours.

If a spare-time income interests you, I strongly recommend that you read my recent book, *How To Build a Second-Income Fortune in Your Spare Time,* Parker Publishing Company, West Nyack, N. Y. Thousands of people have found it laden with golden, magic spare-time wealth ideas. They write me hundreds of letters, saying it has helped them. Pardon my enthusiasm for the book, but as one reader wrote, "It works! If they'd only do what the book says, they'd find that it works, and works!" Try it yourself and see.

CHAPTER 12

Take Smart Money Shortcuts to Wealth

You want to get rich quickly—
at least most people do . . .

Why spend thirty or forty years working eighteen hours a day to build a fortune and then dying before you can enjoy it? No one has yet invented a way to spend money in his grave.

There are magic million-dollar smart money shortcuts you can use in every step of your wealth drive. This chapter shows you what these shortcuts are, and how you can use them. Be sure to put them to work because I want you to be rich within three years. Your chances of achieving this goal are excellent if you use these shortcuts. Here they are.

Check Out Several Possibilities at Once

In earlier chapters you decided which path you'd follow to wealth, a business of your own or a high-pay job. Now you're ready to follow up on either.

Don't investigate one lead at a time. Instead, develop as many leads as possible by

(a) Answering all promising ads
(b) Contacting brokers or employment agencies
(c) Telling people you're looking

Imagine yourself racing for a pot of gold in the form of your own business or a big job. Generate enthusiasm for your goal. "Great designs are not accomplished without enthusiasm of some sort," observed C. N. Bovee, the great editor. "It is the inspiration of everything great."

Make every step you take, every call you make, every idea you have, a positive one. Uncover as many leads as possible in as short a time as possible. The more leads you follow up, the more you'll learn and the quicker will be your education. Resolve today that you'll mount a whirlwind campaign to find a suitable business or job within four weeks. Then get cracking. Don't allow weather, moods, time, family, hobbies, or laziness to stop you. Remember, nothing succeeds like success. So get out and find what you want *today*.

See the Whole Picture Immediately

Train yourself to size up a business or job at a glance. Do this by using these

4 WAYS TO SIZE UP OPPORTUNITIES

(a) Knowing, in advance, exactly what you want
(b) Learning, in advance, the probable dollar range of a business or job
(c) Quickly sizing up the people involved
(d) Comparing asking prices or offered salary with those of another business or job

See with your eyes; hear what people tell you. Train yourself to see and listen intently. Thus, when you first see a place of business you're thinking of buying, use these

6 STEPS IN SIZING UP A BUSINESS

(a) Observe its location. Is it good or bad?
(b) Is the building neat, strong, well kept?
(c) Was the place painted to hide defects?
(d) Are there hidden faults, violations of laws?
(e) Is the customer traffic flow real or rigged?
(f) Could the business *really* earn the claimed income?

This is where you can use your numbers sense. If the owner claims you'll net $2,000 per week in a business, make a quick, easy computation. Ask yourself: *How many customers will have to spend $X to permit me to net the claimed income?* Ask the seller how many customers he has per week and the amount of his average sale. If his *claimed* sales don't agree with your rough estimate, question him more closely.

Look at the seller's account books. *See* them as they actually are. Do they look too clean to have been handled every day for years? People have been known to prepare a false set of books so they could sell a business. Or if the books are dirty, is the dirt real, or was it rubbed into the books to try to fool an observant buyer like yourself? Look, and *see* the truth.

Try to learn where the seller lives. Drive past his house. If you earned the claimed income would you live in this house or a better one? Does the seller drive a big, new car? Does he own more than one car?

Listen to his reason for selling. Does it sound valid (i.e. death of a partner; ill health; other interests; retirement, etc.)? A wise seller will have prepared a valid-sounding reason long before you meet him. Your task is to determine whether the reason is true.

When you're looking for wealth in a job, follow this key rule: *If the prospective employer is unwilling to meet your salary request before you begin working for him, pause and think carefully.* My experience shows that if a firm won't meet your salary request *before* you're hired, there's little chance they'll meet it *after* you're on the payroll. But firms vary, of course, and you'll have to make your own decision.

Evaluate Finances Quickly

Let's say you're thinking of buying a going business. The first one you look at has an asking price of $6,000; the second one, $25,000.

Don't allow the difference of $19,000 to shake you. Instead, ask yourself: "What am I getting for the extra $19,000?" Certainly you should expect to receive

(a) Greater income
(b) Better equipment
(c) More stability
(d) Better location

The $25,000 business may be a better buy than the $6,000 business. Only you can decide this. But do it quickly, by computing the probable income of the business you're considering. Don't spend months on this calculation when minutes are sufficient.

Remember that the average business deals in certain units; pounds, gallons, quarts, hours, etc. If you're looking for a profitable gas station, know in advance that the average gross income per gallon of gasoline sold is 5¢. Then when you find a station selling 100,000 gallons a month, you know immediately that its gasoline gross income is $(0.05)(100,000) = \$5,000$ per month.

Many people first venturing out to find a good business or job are frightened by the big numbers, whether these numbers be in the thousands or the millions. Don't be scared by numbers. They can only help you if you use them correctly. Numbers tell you yes or no—i.e. you should take over this business or job, or you shouldn't.

Learn the numbers of your prospective business by talking to people in the business, reading about the business, and by obtaining statistics from trade associations and other industry groups.

If your mental arithmetic is slow, read a copy of Henry Sticker's *How to Calculate Quickly,* Dover Publications, Inc., New York, N. Y. It will speed up your financial-analysis ability immensely.

Never Pay the Asking Price

I've bought, and sold, several businesses. Hundreds of people I know have done the same. In every case where a business was sold, the seller raised the price *before* putting it on the market. Why? Because he knew the buyer would try to knock down the price before closing the deal. Since a little friendly barter enhances any business deal, the seller usually raises his price 10 to 20 per cent so he has a cushion for bartering without reducing the price he wants to put into his pocket.

In any business purchase keep two facts in mind.

(1) *Have the money and desire to buy the business. Since, in general, there are more sellers than buyers, you, as buyer, have a slight advantage.*

(2) *The seller wants your money. And, in general, he wants to sell the business as quickly as possible with as few problems as possible. So he's usually willing to negotiate the price.*

The seller has one advantage over you, however. He knows exactly how much the business *really* earns. As a prospective buyer you can only guess what the business really earns. But the longer you insist on a lower price, the more the seller *thinks* you know the true income. Since most sellers tend to exaggerate the true income, when they sense that you know the actual income, they are more willing to reduce the price they are asking for the business.

So never pay the asking price! You may lose one or two deals this way but you'll save money and get rich sooner by refusing to pay the asking price for any business.

If you are building wealth through a job, follow this rule. When you apply for a job, ask for the largest salary you think the position will pay. Stick to your requested salary. Don't allow a personnel manager or future boss to convince you to work for less. Becoming rich by working for someone else isn't easy. Therefore, you must set an asking price in advance and stick to it.

Push for a Fast Closing

"It's later than you think," applies to everyone. Why delay a profitable deal when you've make up your mind? Push ahead and close the deal fast.

George Auslander, an architect, turned to mechanical engineering when he found he enjoyed working with machinery designs. While operating a boiler company, he acquired 18 apartment houses in a *brief* time. He held the down payment on each to a nominal amount. His business profits later enabled him to buy an interest in a small bank. Today the bank has twenty branches and George Auslander uses a helicopter to fly from one branch to another. He traces some of his success to his wise acquisition of the apartment houses.

A seller may delay a deal for sentimental reasons, or he may be hoping that a buyer with more money will come along and pay a higher price or make a larger down payment on the business. Don't tolerate delay; push for a quick closing. Here are typical closing times for various business and job deals:

TYPICAL CLOSING TIMES FOR DEALS

(a) Rental real estate	60 days
(b) Retail business (no license needed)	14 days
(c) Retail business (license required)	60-90 days
(d) Top-level job	14-90 days

It can take from two to thirteen weeks to close a deal under normal conditions. If you delay, or the seller or future employer delays, you lose income. Why waste dollars when time is so short? A dollar earned today is worth a little more tomorrow. So get cracking and close that deal.

Be Nice—But Tough

Few people in this world are giving anything away free of charge. In fact, most people are trying to drive the hardest bargain possible. This is as it should be because competition creates business ambition and drive.

Be pleasant, polite, and gentlemanly in your business dealings. Everyone respects, and remembers, a gentleman. *But be tough.* "Nice guys finish last," observed Leo Durocher. You can't win the business battle while keeping everyone happy. Someone, sooner or later, will be displeased. But this is the story of the business world, whether you own your own business or work for someone else.

Stick to your beliefs. You won't always be right; when you're wrong, admit it and change your views. But if you're right, insist on getting what you believe you deserve. This may seem selfish but it does improve your chances of getting what you want. Emerson observed, "Man was born to be rich, or grows rich by the use of his faculties, by the union of thought with nature." When you insist on what you believe is right, you are using your faculties to grow rich.

Be strong and tough. People will respect you for your strength, and will be attracted to you. Business and working for a living aren't popularity contests. Don't try to make them such. You will only lose money and time.

Start Your Business Right

Throughout this book I've recommended that, if you wish to become rich today, you go into business for yourself. J. Paul Getty, said to be the richest, or one of the richest men in the United States, recommends the same. For safety's sake, I recommend that you buy a going business because I think your chances for success are much greater, at least in your first venture.

When you take over a going business, or obtain a top-level job, your chances for success are much greater if you start right. To start right

    (a) Get as much information as possible from the previous owner or job-holder

    (b) Believe and use the information given you by successful owners and workers

    (c) Carefully weigh information presented by unsuccessful owners or workers

Suppose the successful owner tells you, "Don't lend money to the customers—it doesn't pay." You want to be a nice guy and make every customer a friend. So you lend money liberally. Soon, business begins to fall off. The customers who accepted credit no longer show up. You wonder why. Plautus, a Roman poet who lived 200 years before our modern calendar began, said, "If you lend a person money, it becomes lost for any purposes of your own. When you ask for it back again, you find a friend made an enemy by your own kindness."

Use these general rules when taking over a going business:

6 WAYS TO KEEP A BUSINESS STRONG

(a) Don't raise prices immediately
(b) Don't radically change the atmosphere of the business
(c) Don't tolerate abusive customers
(d) Do stop all illegal or shady practices
(e) Do be friendly, helpful
(f) Do work hard and long

When you start a new top-level job, take these steps:

9 STEPS TO JOB SUCCESS

(a) Take charge; don't relinquish command
(b) See and hear what goes on around you
(c) Watch and wait; you learn more
(d) If you don't know, be quiet
(e) If you're sure you know, speak up
(f) Show your authority a few times
(g) "Shake up" the staff with a few rumors
(h) Size up the situation fast
(i) When you're sure you know what you want to do, move ahead at full speed

Hold Expenses Down

When you first buy a new business or obtain a top-level job, and the lovely cash begins to pour in, there's a tendency to think the flow will never end. So some people go out and spend more than they normally would. Take my advice, here and now—*don't do it*. The cash flow may end, or decrease, sooner than you think.

Why may the flow shrink? For many reasons beyond your control. The neighborhood in which you buy the business may be changing; the market for your product may be changing; it may take several months for the people you serve to become accustomed to you. So make every effort to hold your expenses to the minimum possible.

You can reduce your expenses in a business by

(a) Delaying costly major improvements
(b) Stretching out payments for as long as possible
(c) Doing as much work yourself as you can
(d) Laying off unnecessary employees
(e) Finding new ways to save money

In observing hundreds of businessmen my private conclusion is that the most successful are those who hold expenses in line at all times. The very process of continually watching costs leads to a success-oriented outlook. Remember, every dollar you save is an additional dollar in your pocket.

When you take a new top-level job you may have a desire to splurge on new clothes, a sassy new car, and even a new house or apartment. Resist the urge for a few months, until you are comfortably settled into your new position. Then you can calmly look around and decide what you need and want. When you buy under these circumstances you will make wiser purchases, and you'll get more for your money.

"Why do you tell me these things?" you ask. I'm convinced that you'll soon be earning big money; therefore, I want to guide you to complete success.

Big money can do strange things to people. When your wallet is bulging with one-hundred dollar bills you can soon begin to feel like a king. Fine. Keep your wallet in your pocket and wait for a while. Watch to see how things develop. If everything goes as you plan for six months, or longer, loosen up and spend a little. You deserve it for having been so good until now.

Budget Your Income and Outgo

Most of us cringe when we hear the word *budget*. It brings to mind long columns of numbers which are dull, difficult, and destroy pleasure. This is unfortunate because budgets are important keys to success in *every* business or top-level executive job. Most budgets are concerned with money. But some people, salesmen, for example, must budget both time and money. Let's see how you can make budgeting painless and pleasant for yourself.

Budgeting is profit planning. All you need do is estimate your total income for a given period, say one month. Put this at the top of a column. Then estimate your total expenses; rent, electricity, labor, etc., for the same period. Enter these in the same column, thus:

TYPICAL BUDGET FOR A SMALL BUSINESS

Month	November		December	
Income (gross)	Estimated	Actual	Estimated	Actual
	$1,500	1,457	$1,800	1,750
Expenses				
Labor	400	384	420	430
Rent	200	200	200	200
Electricity	30	32	33	31
Taxes	15	15	15	15
Insurance	140	140	140	140
Total	785	771	808	816
Net Income	$ 715	$ 686	$ 992	$ 934

Find the sum of the estimated expenses and subtract them from the estimated gross income. The result is your estimated net income for this period.

At the end of the month enter the actual income and actual expenses, as shown above. Subtract the actual expenses from the actual gross income. The result is your actual net income.

Prepare a budget like this for every month of the year. You can do this in an hour or so for the usual small business. Once your budget is finished you know

(a) Your probable income for each month
(b) Your probable expenses for each month
(c) Your probable net profit for each month

Be sure to vary your budgeted income and expenses from month to month if the income is seasonal. If the months of October through June are the biggest income months, enter the largest income for these months. Enter a smaller income for July through September. Do the same for the expenses, if these vary seasonally.

Budgets give you control and mastery over your financial future. Use budgets in your personal life to control your spending for your childrens' education, your home, and your hobbies. Your chances for outstanding success and great wealth are immensely improved when you use the budget shortcut. You'll never run out of money when you budget carefully.

Be In Control at All Times

Don't depend too much on hired labor in your business when you first start. Be in control at all times. Why? Because when you control a business you

(a) Know exactly what's going on
(b) Learn every important facet of the business
(c) Keep track of the money
(d) Have your own interests constantly in mind

In the various businesses I operate I have had to relinquish some control because I don't have the time to be in complete control at all times. So what I've tried to do is to put one loyal employee in charge. My experience indicates that loyal and honest employees can be found. In general, these employees are

(a) Older; often retired and in their sixties
(b) Strongly religious
(c) Happily married
(d) Willing to work partly on commission

Older women often make very loyal employees. They are honest and dependable.

To avoid stealing, which is really much less common than many people believe, simply make part of the employee's wages commission, or a portion of the day's income. Then the employee wants to work harder to earn more for you so he'll have a larger share for himself.

When I find a loyal employee I make him the boss. I tell him, "You're my man. I'm relying on you to run this show profitably." This gives the employee a feeling of importance. One employee is so loyal that he volunteers to skip his paycheck whenever he has a bad week. (I never allow him to do this.) Another comes to work three hours early sometimes "because maybe I can help." A third does the work of two men because it saves me money.

In working with these older, very loyal employees, I always take their advice. One of them was after me for several months to buy some replacement equipment. I didn't think the equipment was needed immediately but I could see that he wanted it very much. Finally I gave in, saying, "Here's a hundred dollars, Joe. Buy whatever you think we need."

He was delighted; he spent his day off searching for the equipment. Once it was delivered I saw he was right. The new equipment improved business and quickly earned back its cost. And my employee was more loyal than ever because he glowed with the importance of having selected the needed equipment.

When you take over a new top-level job, retain control of all functions for the first few months. If you relinquish control too soon you may find that you delegated authority to the wrong people. So hold the reins tight until you're sure of the job yourself and are sure of your employees. Only then should you delegate control.

Stretch Out Your Debts

There are two schools of thought on managing a debt:

(1) Pay off the debt as soon as possible
(2) Take as long as possible to pay off the debt

Since I started with little in life because my father died when I was twelve, I had to borrow money to make money. It wasn't until later in life that I discovered that the wealthy smart money men in this world did the same. There was a difference, of course. They borrowed money to make money because this is a wise way to expand your money-making abilities. I borrowed because I *had* to; I didn't have a personal fortune to start with.

I assume you don't have much capital and that you use OPM, as recommended in Chapter 6. My experience shows that the biggest problem people face when trying to become rich is that of finding enough capital to buy a business. If they have $1,000 in cash, the kind of business they want costs $10,000, or $20,000. Then, if they borrow the money from several sources, they may have a big monthly payment hanging over their heads.

What to do? One excellent answer is: *stretch out your debts.*

4 ADVANTAGES OF STRETCHED-OUT DEBTS

(a) Stretched-out debts have lower monthly payments
(b) The interest is provable and tax-deductible
(c) You have a higher net profit
(d) You improve your credit rating

Let's say you buy a business on OPM by borrowing $15,000 from banks and signing a $9,000 promissory note given by the seller. Once you take over the business you find that you can pay the bank without trouble. However, the seller's promissory note, on which you must pay $300 per month plus interest, is more difficult to pay. While the business earns enough for you to pay the $300 per month, the burden is more than you want at this time. What can you do?

You can grin and bear it, paying the $300 per month for 30 months until the loan is paid off. This is a valid approach that is used by some businessmen. The principle is, "We'll sweat it out now; when the note is paid off we'll be in clover."

I believe every businessman should sweat out several loan repayments. It's a maturing experience that gives you greater confidence in yourself.

But suppose you don't want to sweat out this note; what then? The answer is: *Use more OPM.* Here's how.

Suppose you borrow $4,000 net on a personal signature

loan. Your payments will be $130 per month for 36 months. Let's assume you've made six payments of $300 each on the note mentioned above. This is a typical situation.

With the $4,000 cash you receive you can make $4,000/300 = 13 and one-third payments on your $300 note. Or. if you wish, you can make 26 and two-third payments of $150 each on the $300 note. Since you've already made six payments on the note, this would carry you past the end of the note payoff period. Your monthly payments would be $150 + $130 = $280, which is $20 per month less than the seller's note payment. This really isn't too much relief.

Your best bet would be to use the $4,000 cash to make 13 payments of the $300 note. Then you need pay only $130 per month, instead of $300 per month, a saving of $170 per month.

At the end of 13 months you will be faced with a payment of $300 + $130 = $430 per month. If business is better at that time, you can make this monthly payment. If business isn't better, you can refinance the $4,000 bank note. You will have repaid $1,690 (= 13 months × $130 per month) on this note, of which about $290 will be interest. Thus, your actual repayment of the loan will be about $1,400. Any bank would lend you this $1,400 plus another $1,000. You would then have $2,400 cash and would owe $2,990 (= 23 month × $130 per month) in addition from the first loan, for a total of $2,400 + $2,990 = $5,390. Your monthly payment on this would be about $175 per month for 36 months.

You have eleven payments of the $300 note remaining (= 30 months − 13 payments − 6 payments). If you wanted, you could make eight payments of $300 each with your $2,400 cash. You would then have only three payments of the note to make. The bank must, of course, be repaid $175 per month for 36 months. This, however, is a manageable payment, compared with $300 per month.

Use Your Cash Wisely

Money has a time value; that is, money in the hand may be worth more than a series of future payments, such as the $300 monthly note mentioned above. So when you borrow a sum of several thousand dollars, go to the note holder and ask him if he'd sell you more than thirteen notes for $4,000. He may need money so badly that he'll be willing to sell sixteen or eighteen notes for the price of thirteen. This is not a dishonest practice; it is done frequently in both small and large businesses.

Guard your cash wisely. Don't allow it to go to your head. If you hold the cash you borrow, deposit it in a savings bank. This cash will earn interest in the savings bank. The interest will help repay some of the interest you must pay on the bank loan. Withdraw enough cash from the savings bank each month to pay the monthly note, or half of it, depending on which method of payment you chose. Keep in mind at all times the advice of a famous millionaire. He said, "When you're poor, cash is scarce; when you're rich you try to make your cash scarce so others won't take it away from you."

Expand When You Have the Opportunity

In my main field of business we often invest money in a new idea soon after the idea first develops. A few months later someone else may come along with an obviously better idea. Then we have a problem. Should we invest in both ideas, or run with just the first?

We usually invest in both ideas. Why? Because the first idea may not pay off, and the second may, or vice versa. By investing in both ideas we have a double chance of hitting the big money. If we back only one idea it may be the wrong one.

You may run into a similar situation in business this way. A business appeals to you and, after thorough investigation, you buy it. Several months later a similar business becomes available. If you have the same luck I do, the second business will earn a greater income than the first, and will cost less. What should you do? Take several steps.

1. *Evaluate the second business.* Since you are already in the same business, you know what profit you might expect. You also know your *true* expenses. These are often difficult to estimate accurately before you buy a business.

2. *Figure if the income from the second business would help the first.* The first business you buy may generate only half or three-quarters the income you anticipated. Will the same happen with the second? Or is it so much better than the first business that it will help pay it off? This happened to me once; the second business I bought helped me pay off the first. Later, the first business improved to the point where its income equalled that of the second.

3. *Imagine the worst that could happen.* Suppose you lost both businesses. What then? Could you pay off the debts you have? Suppose only one business went bad. Would the income from the other pay the debts you'd have? Sit down with pencil and paper and figure out the worst that could happen.

4. *Make your decision.* Take your time. Be certain of what your doing. Figure and re-figure, as necessary. Once you make up your mind, push ahead, using the shortcuts you learned in this chapter.

Make Your Job Pay Off

A friend of mine earns $18,000 per year. "Last year," he told me, "I brought in $2,250,000 worth of new business to our company.. Thus, I obtained $125 in business for every dollar the company paid me. I feel I should be paid more."

"Let's take a closer look," I said. "Of the $125 you brought in, how much was profit?"

He thought for a while; then he said, "About $10 to $12."

"Now do you still think you should be paid more?" I asked.

"No; not on the basis of $10 to $12 profit per $1 of salary," he said.

Recognize, here and now, that your salary is tied, directly or indirectly, to the business you bring to your company. The more business you bring in, the greater your potential earnings.

So if you want to get rich on a job, find the business and bring it in.

Sometimes you can find business before the company does. Tom K. developed an easy way to pump chemicals. He found several large companies that were willing to pay big money for his method. With their orders in his pocket he applied for a job at several pump companies. None of the companies were too interested until he showed them the orders. Then they all jumped to hire him. He accepted a position as vice-president of engineering at a salary of $50,000 per year. Today he's president of a pump company because he makes his job pay off.

You can do the same, if you find the business, either before or after you have the big job. Know your business and where to find it and you can succeed in a big way.

Use Shortcuts Carefully

Throughout this chapter I've urged you to use shortcuts whenever possible. But using shortcuts doesn't mean you should make snap decisions. Some snap decisions are correct; many are incorrect. *Nothing can replace careful analysis with a pencil and paper.*

So know what you're doing—before you do it. Then use every one of these shortcuts to the utmost.

CHAPTER **13**

Magic Secrets That Zoom Your Income

No matter how you decide
to build your riches ...

...in a business of your own, or on a job, you will often have to take action to increase your income. If you sit back and wait for more business to come to you, or for the boss to give you a raise, your wait may be a long one. In this chapter you'll learn many secrets that will zoom your income to top figures.

Be Ready for the Worst

"That's negative thinking," you say.

I'd rather call it positive-negative thinking because by being ready for the worst you prepare for the best. And since I want you to have all of the best in life, you should be ready to take any steps necessary to obtain it. One of these steps is to be ready for the worst. Why?

Because the worst *can* happen. A business can fail. You can be fired from a top-level job; many people have been. By being ready for the worst, you remove almost all the fear that accompanies an unknown situation. You also improve your chances for overcoming the worst.

How can you prepare for the worst? That's easy. Sit down with a pencil and paper and list the worst that could happen to you and your business or job. Here's a list Paul D., a young business owner, prepared.

WORST-HAPPENINGS LIST

HAPPENING	ACTION TO TAKE
1. Business income decreases	1. Hold special sales; reduce labor force
2. Business fails to pay its expenses	2. Sell business to recover investment
3. Sale of business doesn't pay off the investment in it	3. Take a job and use part of the income to pay off debts
4. Illness hits me	4. Obtain a liberal health insurance policy
5. I die or am killed	5. Maintain a large enough life insurance policy

This list might apply to almost any business. Study it carefully; you may find several ideas which would be useful in planning your own business.

Here's a job worst-happenings list which Gary K., a young executive, prepared. It shows good planning.

WORST-HAPPENING LIST

HAPPENING	ACTION TO TAKE
1. Demoted on my job	1. Accept; look for new job elsewhere
2. No pay raises offered	2. Insist on a raise; if not given, resign after finding new job
3. No promotion offered	3. Ask for promotion; resign after finding new job
4. Laid off	4. Ask for severance pay; find new job
5. Fired	5. Ask for use of company facilities while finding new job
6. I die or am killed	6. Maintain a large enough insurance policy

Buy the Protection You Need

You can buy much of the protection you need in a business or a job. Thus, you can buy

(a) *Fire insurance*—pays your losses from fire
(b) *Liability insurance*—pays people hurt in your business place
(c) *Business interruption insurance*—pays you while business is stopped
(d) *Health insurance*—pays you a salary while you're sick
(e) *Hospitalization insurance*—pays your hospital bills
(f) *Life insurance*—pays the business if you die or are killed
(g) *Auto and truck insurance*—pays costs when you have an accident.

"How can these zoom my income?" you ask.

Having this insurance coverage makes you more relaxed. You never worry about the place burning down, someone tripping on a step, or a large hospital bill. Your insurance covers all these. So you work without worry, and do a better job. Best of all, the cost of this insurance is legally deductible on your income tax. The freedom of mind you obtain costs very little and its effect is many hundreds of times worth its cost.

Get yourself a good insurance agent and show him your worst-happenings list. Ask him how he can protect you against most of the happenings. He'll be glad to provide the protection you need at low cost. Be ready for the worst, even though the worst seldom happens, and your income can zoom in a relaxed and safe atmosphere.

Have Extra Cash Handy

I began to live my business life on the basis of two axioms:

(1) Everything in business costs more than you figure
(2) Everything in business takes longer than you think it should

So far, after years of experience in several businesses, I haven't met a situation which proved these two axioms wrong.

That's why you should always have some cash handy. If you're paying $10,000 for a business, borrow $12,000. Keep the extra $2,000 in a savings account for a year. You'll earn interest and you'll be ready for those unpredictable bills that almost every business faces in its early life.

Steven Bains opened a small, intimate restaurant on the west side of Manhattan. He serves good food to a mixed group; publishing executives, merchant captains and officers, garment-firm owners, etc. The restaurant has an attractive European-New York waterfront atmosphere.

Recently Steve saw an ad for an auction of the supplies of the luxury liner *America,* after she had been sold to Greek owners. Steve attended the auction with some extra cash in his pocket. He was able to buy some excellent items; silver corn holders at 1¢ a pair; silver spoons, 7¢ each; silver dessert knives, 10¢ each.

His customers delight in using these attractive silver utensils that once were part of a world-famous vessel. Steve was able to get these excellent bargains for just one reason; he keeps some extra cash handy at all times.

Publicize What You Do

People everywhere respect, and believe, the printed word. You can publicize your business in many ways, using the printed word. What's more, it will cost you very little to obtain effective publicity in print. Here's how.

Magazines and newspapers run regular columns on what's new in products, clothes, toys, books, and hundreds of other items. All you need do is send a glossy photograph of your item and a single-page doubled-spaced condensed description of it. Give all pertinent facts; size, color, materials, weight, and price.

Send these new product releases to every magazine and newspaper whose readers might be interested in your item. You'll be delighted with the free space the magazine or newspaper devotes to your product. Many orders may pour into your office.

You have a service, not a product? Find some special aspect of your service which is different from all your competitors. Feature this special aspect in your release. Or hold an open house for the public. Send an announcement to the newspapers, giving the time and date of your show. Point out what the public will gain by attending; increased knowledge, a behind-the-scenes view of the workings of the service, and special low prices that you may be offering for the duration of the show.

Sometimes a magazine or newspaper editor will come after you to obtain a story about your product. Recently the editor of a big city daily wrote a long, illustrated story about Jack Bodi and Joseph Leombruno, two successful fashion photographers. They moved to Italy and opened a photo studio in Rome. As a sideline, they put some knitting machines in the space above their studio and soon had women turning out knitwear fashions. They called their line Micia, meaning little cat.

When they opened their first American factory, their line was described as "the raciest knit dresses this side of the Via Veneto." The article showed a picture of Jack Bodi with a mannequin wearing one of the knitted dresses. Prices of the dresses; $30 to $50, sizes; 3 to 13, and probable age range of the wearers; 18 to 40, were all given in the article.

Publicity serves a valid and useful function throughout the world today. Use publicity whenever you can. The time and energy you spend at it will be repaid many times over.

The value of publicity was brought out to me recently while I was dining at the *Four Seasons* in New York. A prominent businessman asked me about condominium apartment ownership. I gave a brief answer to the question.   ,

"Is there a good book on the subject?" was his next question.

"Yes," I said. "There was a book on condominiums described in last Sunday's *Times* real-estate section. It was written by Daniel S. Berman, the well-known author. From what the notice said, this book covers every aspect of condominiums."

"That's just what I need. Did the article give the price of the book?"

"Yes, it did," I said. "The price is $50."

"It must be good," the businessman said. "I'll order a copy this afternoon."

Thus, a short (5-inch) item about a good book easily sold a copy. Now do you question the value of publicity?

Use Publicity in a Job or Profession

You can approach your job or profession as though it were a small business and publicize your activities. This publicity will put you in a favorable light with your supervisors.

You can use the same technique if you are in a profession; a consulting engineer, economist, dentist, etc. Simply publicize your activities in the various journals, magazines, newspapers, etc., serving your profession.

Eleven Steps to Good Job or Profession Publicity

Here's a useful and profitable program you can apply in almost any job or profession.

1. *List the journals, magazines, and newspapers in your field* and in closely related fields. If you don't know all of them,

consult *Standard Rate and Data* in any library. This gives a complete list.

2. *Study several copies of each publication.* Note what kinds of contributed material they use from outside authors. Are illustrated articles, short how-to kinks, personal experience stories, or other types of material most popular? Or are all popular?

3. *Decide which type of material you will prepare.* Choose the type of material that appeals to you most, and the publication in which you would like to have it appear. Select a second publication that might use the material if the first doesn't want it.

4. *Prepare the material.* Relax, don't act as though you're writing the great American novel. Tell your "story" in simple, clear language. Avoid big words, except where they are a part of the vocabulary of your job or profession.

5. *Use a standard format.* Prepare your material in the same format as the material in the publication you've chosen. Thus, if you decided to write an illustrated article, prepare the title; the "blurb", i.e., the short summary of the article which appears under the title; the text; the illustrations. Use the same type of subheads as the publication. Usually they are centered or lead-in types.

6. *"Package" your material.* Most publications have several standard-length pieces they use. Count the words in a number of articles or other items and try to make your material about the same length. Count the number of illustrations, and the type, photo or drawing. Try to use about the same number of illustrations in your article or release.

7. *Send your material to the editor.* Don't bother writing a letter asking him if he wants your material. Instead, send your material, typed double-space on only one side of good bond paper, to the editor with a short letter explaining why you think his readers will like your article or release, what qualifications you have for writing it, and why you chose his magazine. If you can't find the editor's name on the magazine, just address your letter to The Editor. You need not enclose return postage; most magazines and newspapers abandoned this requirement long ago.

8. *Wait for the editor to write you.* You'll receive either a letter of acceptance or a rejection within four to eight weeks if you submitted an article. News and product releases are hardly

ever acknowledged. Just watch future issues of the publication for the item. If the item is suited to the magazine or newspaper, the chances that it will be published are excellent. When an editor doesn't acknowledge an article within eight weeks, drop him a postcard asking what happened.

9. *Reprint the published item.* Buy copies of the published item from the magazine or newspaper and send these copies to friends in the organization you work for and to other people who might be interested in the item. You can also make photocopies of the article for limited, free distribution.

10. *Send news and product releases to many publications.* Every magazine and newspaper in the field will welcome your news and product releases. There isn't any competition amongst publications for these items. But send articles, how-to kinks, and similar editorial items to only one magazine or newspaper. If your material is accepted for publication, you may be paid at rates up to $50 per published page. If your material is rejected, you can send it to any other magazine of your choice. That's why I recommend that you choose two, or more, publications to whom you plan to send the material (Step 3).

11. *Prepare a scrapbook of your published items.* Buy a scrapbook having clear plastic pages. Insert each published item in the scrapbook. Your scrapbook can be a valuable sales tool that can be used in almost any business activity. So make use of it whenever you can!

Publicity Can Make Money for You

During my consultations with ambitious men and women I introduce them to the principles of publicity you just learned. Most of these people are amazed to learn they can get free publicity in magazines and newspapers. And when they hear they may be paid for writing items that publicize their own products or activities, they can't wait to get to a desk and start writing.

But the main purpose of publicity is to spread the word about yourself, your product, or your organization. So concentrate on this aspect of publicity because it will usually bring you a greater return than the payment you receive for an article. The benefits of free publicity are greater than you could ever imagine.

A friend of mine, Cal T., owned a laundry. He came to me and asked how he could publicize his laundry. I suggested articles in the local paper, a plant tour, backing a Little League team, a family picnic, and similar ideas. He jumped at these ideas and soon had his laundry's name spread all over town. Business boomed.

Owners of several laundries in nearby towns heard about Cal's success. They asked him to publicize their laundries. At first he was reluctant; then he agreed. Soon Cal was preparing publicity for laundries throughout the state. The local trade association of laundry owners recommended Cal to both prosperous and not-so-prosperous owners.

One evening about a year ago I met Cal in the theatre lobby between the acts of a new Broadway musical.

"How's it going?" I asked.

"Great," he said. "But I have problems."

"Oh? What kind of problems?"

"Money problems. The income from my publicity work is now greater than from the laundry. Because of that I'm spending more time on publicity than on the laundry."

"Why not start a public-relations agency?"

"That's just what I've been thinking of doing," Cal said. The second act began before we could talk more.

Cal sold his laundry and opened a public-relations agency. Today he has ten clients and he could have one hundred if he wanted. Cal charges each client $10,000 per year and works 24 days per year, about one-half a day per week, for each client. Cal's income is $100,000 per year and he works five days per week, with a one-month vacation.

Recently I asked Cal why he didn't take on more clients.

"Because one-hundred grand a year is an ideal income. I couldn't spend any more. I have a beautiful home overlooking Long Island Sound. Two brand-new Caddies sit in my driveway. And I own the sweetest forty-foot Chris-Craft a man ever saw. So why kill myself?"

Truly, the benefits of publicity can be greater than you ever imagined!

Advertise Your Business

You can publicize a business free of charge for about two years. Then you have to think about advertising, unless your product or service has a relatively short selling period. Eugene Feldman, an outstanding artist-lithographer-printer, recently produced a beautiful 25-foot panoramic folder of New York's West Side using nine multi-color offset impressions. This excellent collector's item was issued in a limited edition of 250 copies, signed and numbered, at $50 each. The demand for this attractive and original folder will probably be so great that Mr. Feldman will never have to advertise it. Publicity alone will quickly sell it out.

On the other hand, a ship-model builder, Rene K., advertises regularly because he builds a variety of ship models ranging in price from $100 to $2,000 each. His products are as varied as the ships that have sailed the seas since the beginning of time. In each model he uses the same lumber and metals as were used in the original ships. To keep people informed about the new models he has available, Rene advertises in magazines and newspapers that are read by people who are interested in decorative models and can pay the prices he charges.

Advertising costs money but it can zoom your income because it

(a) Keeps your product in public view

(b) Builds a favorable image for your business

(c) Creates a desire for your product

(d) Establishes brand-name loyalty

(e) Can double or triple sales

Choose the Best Form for Advertising

You can advertise in many ways. Here are ten ways you might advertise the products or services of a growing business:

10 VALUABLE ADVERTISING METHODS

(1) Signs inside and outside the place of business
(2) Newspaper and magazine ads
(3) Telephone-book yellow-page ads
(4) Mailed announcements of new items
(5) Hand-distributed leaflets
(6) Printed match covers
(7) Printed glass and plate coasters
(8) Engraved pens, pencils, gifts
(9) Calendars, desk pads, blotters, rulers
(10) Catalogs, brochures, flyers

Study this ten-item list to find one or more ways you might use to advertise your business. When you first buy or start a business you usually don't have enough money to pay for newspaper or magazine ads, brochures, etc. So you have to choose lower-cost ways to advertise your business or product.

My experience with growing businesses shows that these ways of advertising are cheapest:

(a) Inside and outside signs—make them yourself
(b) Hand-distributed leaflets—print from a low-cost stencil
(c) Mailed announcements—address and mail yourself
(d) Telephone book yellow-page ads—cost only pennies per month

Make the Public Aware of Your Product or Service

When you buy a business that has been operating for many years, the owner is usually comfortably rich. You'll often find that he allowed advertising to taper off in the last few years because this is an easy way to save money. He wanted to enjoy his riches.

Your first few months in the business may be good and then sales begin to decline. Why? During the first few months you had the carryover business from the former owner. But with business declining you wonder what you should do. The best answer is *advertise!* Yet most beginning businessmen cut advertising when sales are poor because they want to save money. *But long exper-*

ience shows that the time to advertise is when business is slow; the time to cut back advertising is when business is good.

Plaster signs all over the inside and outside of your place of business. Paint them yourself, using paper, cardboard, masonite, or plywood. A commercial sign painter will charge you about $2 per square foot to paint a sign made of masonite or plywood. You can paint the same sign yourself for about 25¢ per square foot, including the cost of the paint and wood.

Shine flashing lights on the outdoor signs if your business is open at night. Buy a simple flasher for 40¢ at a hardware store. It will last for years and will get people to look at your sign. Several flashers can give the effect of rotating lights. Rig the lights and flasher using wires plugged into convenient outlets. Once your business earns a big income you can switch to neon signs built by professionals.

Paint indoor signs on white cardboard. Use colorful paints; red, orange, green, etc. Put in stars, rockets, exclamation marks, and other symbols that call attention to the sign. Make your signs big and bold; the more attention they attract the larger your sales.

Become an Ad Printer

All you need is a typewriter, a few stencil blades, and a board. With a little practice you can cut many simple designs in stencils. Al Grover, known as the Chris-Craft King, makes wide use of stencils to prepare useful leaflets that are important in selling boats ranging in price from $500 to $35,000. Yet Al's crew needs nothing more than a few simple items to accomplish this.

Distribute your leaflets in your place of business. Where home sales are important, pay teenagers a nominal fee to distribute your leaflets. Don't worry about the kids throwing the leaflets in the sewer. Long experience with today's teenagers has taught me that they are usually reliable, honest and ambitious. They will be happy to work for you and will turn in a superior performance.

Get Into Mail Order

Mail order is the world's most convenient business. You work at home, in congenial surroundings. If you want to go deep-sea fishing in the morning, you can do your mail order work in the afternoon or evening. Or you can work in the morning, play tennis in the afternoon, and go bowling at night. Take your choice.

You can sell almost anything by mail order. One large Texas store sells airplanes by mail order. Baby elephants are even sold through the mail. Prices of mail-order products range from less than one dollar to many thousands of dollars.

In the early months of your business you can use mail order to both advertise and sell your products. If you make several sales with one mailing, you may recover all, or part, of the mailing cost from the profit earned on the products sold. Then the advertising for the products, which the mailing provides, will be free of charge.

Where you operate a service business such as dry-cleaning, bowling, tavern, etc., you can't expect to sell products through the mail. But your mailing pieces will encourage people to come to your place of business and buy. Some service businesses use local voter lists for their mailings. The money spent by the customers you obtain will repay your investment in the mailing. Two useful mail-order books you should read are:

> E. Joseph Cossman, *How I Made $1,000,000 in Mail Order*, Prentice-Hall, Inc.
>
> Julian L. Simon, *How to Start and Operate a Mail Order Business*, McGraw-Hill Book Company

Advertise; Advertise; Advertise

Every successful firm I know is a big advertiser. The founders of Yarway Corporation developed high-quality valves and other equipment. But the product that really put them "on the map" was a unique steam trap, a device to drain hot water from pipes. Their product was excellent but the buying public had to be convinced. Yarway's founders turned to widespread and helpful advertising. Through good times and bad, they advertised. Their sales grew and grew to the point where today they are one of the world's largest builders of steam traps. The company still advertises regularly and generally uses full-page or spread ads.

Regular advertising needn't be expensive. If a two-line $3

classified ad will do the job, then use it. But run it regularly in the magazine and newspapers your potential customers will read.

Advertising is like saving money. If you save regularly, you quickly build a sizeable sum. But if you save only when the mood is upon you, it takes a long time to accumulate a large sum. And, usually, the person gives up before he has a large account.

Advertise regularly and you will steadily build customers. Advertise irregularly and you lose much of the punch your ads should have.

Be Payment Wise

With a steady, strong, zooming income from your business you can sit back and survey your growing wealth. You'll soon find that when *you* are raking in the income, people will beat a path to your door. Salesmen, bank representatives, stock brokers, insurance men, and a long list of others will be knocking on your door. For, as the ancients remarked, "Money answereth all things."

Money in the bank will give you certain privileges. You should use these privileges, because you are quickly becoming one of the smart money people in this world. Here are eight privileges you should use:

1. *Take the full 10- or 15-day grace period in loan repayments.* It costs you nothing and you have the money in your hands longer.

2. *Pay bills on the first of the following month.* Gas, electric, rent, and similar bills are often marked Payable When Received. Don't rush to pay. Consolidate all your bill payments so you make them at the end of the month. As a good customer, you're entitled to this leeway.

3. *Pay cash where you can get a discount.* Many suppliers offer a 2 per cent discount for cash payment on delivery or within 10 days. Look at it this way—you wouldn't earn this 2 per cent if your money was in a savings account unless the interest was compounded daily, and this is most unusual.

4. *Establish checking and savings accounts in several banks.* With money to spare, you should spread it around. Banks love new accounts. And they are partial to their customers. So

instead of dropping all your money in one bank, use three or four. Then you'll have this many sources of capital when you need it.

5. *Establish a line of credit with one or more banks.* You may never use your line of credit but it will improve your credit rating and provide a quick and easy source of funds in emergencies.

6. *Prepay insurance bills if you can save money by doing so.* For most growing businesses the saving is only a few dollars, unless you require large insurance coverage. Then the saving can make prepayment worthwhile.

7. *Investigate with your bank the best way to invest surplus funds for short periods.* There are many different ways you can invest your extra money so it earns interest. Don't shrug off interest because it amounts to only a few dollars. This is *not* the way to get rich. Chase, and earn, every dollar you can.

8. *Maintain a top-notch credit-rating.* One of the surest ways to slow your climb to riches is by damaging your credit rating. *A bad credit rating can lead to loan-application rejections, high interest rates, and other difficulties. So pay your bills in full on time.*

Keep Your Employees Loyal

The loyal employee is honest, dependable, ambitious, willing, and enthusiastic. He does a good job for you because you take care of him. Plan on making your employees loyal and you have a much better chance of getting rich in business. Neglect your employees and they will neglect your business because by doing so they know, subconsciously, that they are neglecting you. Loyal employees can zoom your income while you sleep. So take action now to build loyalty.

Use these four ways to build loyalty in all your employees:

1. *Pay the highest wages you can.* Make it worthwhile for your employees to come to work. Be sure to point out how your wages compare with those paid by other firms.

2. *Use incentives wherever you can.* Set sales and other performance goals with the employee. Then pay a bonus when he achieves or exceeds his goals. Cut him in on the profits and he will work twice as hard for you.

3. *Know your employees.* Learn as much as you can about each employee, his family, hobbies, ambitions. Keep these facts in mind when you deal with each employee.

4. *Insist on a full day's work.* Don't allow your employees to coast. Be firm but kind. Employees respect the firm but fair employer.

Devise Foolproof Cash Controls

There are many excellent businesses you might buy; a liquor store, a 5- and 10-cent store, a grocery, etc. Almost all retail stores involve daily handling of cash. This can become a problem, particularly when you have new employees.

Use numbered invoices, cash slips, time control cards, and similar records related to cash. Assign employees to different jobs for a week or two every three months. The change in assignment will broaden each employee's skill while permitting you to detect abnormal changes in your cash income.

Be just as alert for dishonesty amongst long-time employees as with new personnel. Some of the largest thefts are committed by employees who have been on the payroll for thirty years or more.

Double-check all cash transactions by having each employee's work examined by another. Install modern cash registers. Where possible, use the type of cash register that prints the amount on the bill of sale. Consider using a removable label on each piece of merchandise. Have the clerk remove this label when the sale is completed. Attach the label to your copy of the sales slip. This procedure, combined with regular checking of your inventory, will prevent thefts from going undetected.

Collect all sales slips every day. Do not allow any vouchers of any kind to remain in the hands of the cash-dispensing clerk longer than one week. Be especially careful with petty-cash vouchers; they can be altered with ease.

Visit a store selling cash registers. You will find that the manager will give you many free hints on controlling cash. He will also provide you with booklets published by firms manufacturing business machines. These booklets contain hundreds of useful ideas on cash control.

You can prevent abuse of your cash income. Follow the hints here and more of your income will stay in your hands.

Save Bill-Collection Steps and Time

Peter F. operates a prosperous health club near me. He has a gym, swimming pool, Swedish massage room, tennis court, and steam bath on his property.

"My income would be great," Pete laughs, "if my customers paid their bills. This health club is in the most exclusive part of town. But I can't get people to pay their bills! How can a guy make a buck under these conditions?"

Pete's problem, like that of many other growing businesses, is not a lack of customers. He has plenty of customers. But too many don't pay their bills on time, or at all.

We discussed Pete's problem one night after attending a performance of the New York Metropolitan Opera.

"Pete," I said, "there's only one way to handle people like this; you have to be nice, but tough!"

"You can't be tough with these people," he said. "They come from the best families in this area."

"Pete, the longer you're in business the more you'll realize that all people, rich and poor, respect the businessman who demands that he be paid. Now get tough with these people and insist that they bay their bills."

Pete took this advice. He sent out notices telling his customers they couldn't use the club until after they paid all outstanding bills. At the start he lost some customers but his cash income increased! Soon he had new customers in place of the non-paying ones he lost. The new ones joined the health club with the understanding that they would pay their bills on the first of the month, when due.

To ensure steady and strong growth of your business:

(a) Keep credit to a minimum, except with standard credit cards (American Express, Esso, etc.)
(b) Never lend cash to your customers; you'll lose both a customer and a friend.

(c) Insist on payment on delivery or when the service is rendered. When a customer runs out of money, be nice but tough. Insist that he pay his bill the next day or as soon as he has the money.

(d) Keep the financial details of your business to yourself. The less the customer knows about your income and profits, the easier it will be for you to do business with him.

(e) Collect bills by mail whenever possible. Thus you'll save time and energy by collecting rent, service bills, professional fees, and similar bills by mail. Use a stamped, addressed return envelope for easy processing by the customer.

(f) Hire a collection agency for large, difficult-to-collect bills. While the agency will charge you a fee, your income will be higher than if the bill goes uncollected.

You can reduce your bad debts to almost nil if you follow these hints. Why lose income when, with some planning, you can collect the money due you? Combine low bad debts with easy collection procedures and you can zoom your income, year after year.

Get Good Tax Advice

You can be earning $25,000 per year in your own business and, with good tax advice, can have more dollars left at the end of the year than a salaried man earning $40,000 per year. As my tax adviser said to me once, "A dollar saved in taxes is a tax-free dollar!"

When you have your own business you are entitled to many legal deductions which a salaried man usually cannot take. By making full, legal use of these deductions you can finish each year with more dollars in your pocket than if you just hastily fill out your tax return without competent advice.

Hire your tax consultant *before* you buy a business. His services will cost you a few dollars, $50 to $100, but they will be worth every penny because your tax savings will be so great. Have your tax consultant advise you on:

1. *The best form for your business.* Sometimes a sole proprietorship is a much better form than a corporation because the tax requirements are fewer.

2. *The importance of a valid noncompetitive clause.* By including a clause whereby the former owner of the business promises not to compete, as part of the purchase contract, you can save many dollars in taxes. The amount of the purchase price which is paid for the noncompetitive clause can be written off over a period specified in the clause, usually five to ten years.

3. *The value assigned to equipment.* You are allowed to depreciate equipment used to produce your income. This reduces the taxes you must pay. Since equipment can be valued in various ways, have your tax consultant choose the best way for you.

4. *The best way to pay off notes.* You are allowed to deduct interest. Promissory notes can be arranged so the interest is paid in various ways. Have your tax consultant choose the best way, and time, for you to pay the interest.

There are hundreds of other legitimate deductions which you can take when you own your own business. A good tax consultant will guide you through the maze of local and national tax laws. With expert help your business will grow, year after year, adding to your wealth.

CHAPTER 14

Reinvest Your Profits for Greater Income

Every wealthy man I know is active in at least two money-making endeavors . . .

Some are in six activities; others are in a dozen. How do they get into so many activities? By branching out, once they acquire an overwhelming desire for wealth. You can do the same, if you reinvest your profits for a greater income.

Look for Greater Income

Some people are easily satisfied in this life. All they want is a job that will pay them a certain weekly salary—say $200— and their ambitions end. Other people are never satisfied; they're always seeking more income.

You can take either course in life. We're not here to discuss which course brings greater happiness. But I do want you to get rich if it will make you happy. So I'm assuming that it will take at least $2,000 per week, and possibly more, to make you completely happy.

Let's say you followed many of the hints in the earlier chapters of this book and that you now have a lucrative business or top-paying job. One day you sit back and say to yourself, "What next? Do I go on earning about the same income for the next ten or fifteen years or do I go out and look for more?" The only answer, if you want to get rich, is to go out and look for more.

The aggressive wealth seeker is an alert, intelligent person who wants more of the good things for himself and his family. I find him more interesting and more stimulating than the man who settles for a modest salary in a routine job. The wealth seeker has more zest, usually knows more, travels further, and has wider interests. He looks for greater income everywhere he goes. Why? Because he recognizes that allowing profits to sit in the bank where they earn about 4 per cent interest is wasteful when the same funds could be earning 8 or 12 per cent when invested wisely. Or, if he's a smart money man, he might seek a 33 per cent return.

What to Look for in Income Sources

There are many tried and proven ways to invest extra funds for greater income. Since you are already reasonably busy with your present business or job, you'll have to be careful when you choose your next source of income. You want a business that will return maximum profit with a minimum investment of your time.

You might invest in the stock market and spend four hours per year supervising your portfolio; or, you might pay a broker to manage your holdings for you. Then the only time you'll spend on your investments is a monthly phone call to your broker.

There are many other factors you must consider when looking for new income sources. These factors are:

(a) *Time*—invest the minimum time possible
(b) *Supervision*—seek a simple business using unskilled labor
(c) *Accounting*—look for a simple cash business with little bookkeeping
(d) *Inventory*—avoid large inventories
(e) *Fragile products*—stay away from easily broken products
(f) *Labor force*—avoid large labor forces requiring much supervision

When you study these factors you quickly realize that only certain businesses will meet your requirements. Note, also, that these requirements apply whether your main activity is a business of your own or a top executive job.

Twelve Good Ways to Reinvest Your Profits

Here are twelve ways to reinvest your income which meet the six requirements listed above. Each of these works well for several successful people I know. Read through these to find one or more activities that may work for you.

Liquor stores require little time and supervision. Accounting is simple; you just count bottles. Inventory needn't be large, except around the holidays when it moves out fast. Liquor and wine bottles are stronger than you think; try to break one and see. One man can run a typical store which is open six days a week, noon to 9 p.m. Profits can be high; thus a typical store, in a moderate-rent district, having annual liquor sales of $200,000 will net $30,000 per year profit, or 15 per cent. As one owner puts it, "People aren't allowed to drink on the premises so you don't have any trouble with them. Also, all sales are cash on the barrelhead!"

Rental real estate can be an ideal source of additional income. With good management you needn't spend more than two hours per week supervising the property. Your accounting is simple; there is no inventory; the product, an apartment, is strong and solid. The labor force is small; one or two men. To achieve success in rental real estate, aim high; buy the largest building you can. A 50-apartment building will pay higher profits with greater security than a 20-apartment building. Labor costs are lower and there's less danger from loss of tenants. Rental apartments will usually pay you 10 to 30 per cent net profit on your *cash* investment while paying off the property. You can borrow the cash needed for the down payment and thus operate completely on OPM (Chapter 6). One real-estate investor remarked to me, "Some tenants will drive you nuts but those rent checks on the first of the month are marvelous medicine!"

Beauty salons are immensely busy these days, require little supervision, have simple accounting, minimum inventory, and little labor. Fully equipped stores are reasonable, usually costing less than $5,000. With a $700-per-week income you should net $200 per week. Why? Because the ingredients for a $20 permanent cost less than $1. Find several good hairdressers and you can get rich on your extra profits.

Parking lots are the simplest business in today's automobile-mad world. One or two young auto lovers can operate a lot with hardly any supervision from you. Accounting is simple; you have no inventory; the product, rental of a piece of land for a few hours, is certainly not fragile. You either can buy or lease a parking lot. Since the price of land has been increasing since the beginning of recorded time, a parking lot that just pays its expenses (called a tax-payer) is often regarded as profitable because the land is going up in value. So if you own the land you may eventually be able to sell out at a profit. A good downtown parking lot in a large city should net $10,000 to $100,000 per year, depending on the lot size and the parking rates.

Summer camps often gross $100,000 per year and, with good management, can be highly profitable. By using school teachers and college students to run the camp for you, the time and energy you invest can be held to a minimum. "Sometimes those screaming kids get to me," notes one camp owner, "but then I think of the fee the kids' parents are paying (usually $700 to $1,000 for seven weeks) and I can put up with anything. You might call me a very high-priced baby sitter!"

Model raceways, where kids race small electric cars, are

booming. The sale of cars, controls, spare parts, and refreshments can account for 60 per cent of the gross income; track rental income accounts for the balance. Time, supervision, accounting, and labor are minimal. You should, however, be promotion-minded because this is a business requiring active advertising in the local area. As with summer camps, you are a high-priced baby-sitter. But the income that flows into your pocket is real and the bank won't ask you where it came from. Neither will the auto dealer when you stroll in to buy your first full-size shiny new Cadillac.

Billiard rooms today are much different from the smoke-filled dimly lit pool rooms of the past. Today's billiard rooms have wall-to-wall carpeting, brightly lit tables, and vending machines for food and drinks. You can operate a typical billiard room with only two attendants, little supervision and accounting. There is hardly any inventory and billiard balls seldom break. A 20-table room charging a basic rate of $1.80 per hour should gross about $75,000 per year and net $25,000 to $30,000 per year, depending on your rent and labor costs. You needn't visit the room more than once a week to take a look around. This business has been particularly lucrative for me and I (a) am the world's worst billiard player, (b) don't have time to spend in billiard rooms, and (c) hardly ever go near the places.

Hero shops serving Italian-style hero sandwiches are popular in large and small towns and cities. The food is simple; you don't need a hotel chef to prepare it. Depending on the size of the shop, you need two to five employees. Your manager supervises the help. All you need do is stop by now and then to check on the food and cleanliness of the place. A lawyer friend of mine owns a hero shop on a New York side street. This shop, with five employees, grosses more than $1,000 per day. The owner's net is $200 per day. As he says, "I have a good manager. He runs an efficient shop. So I leave him alone. Can you name me an easier way to net $200 per day, five days a week without working in the place?" I can't; can you?

Stock-market investments can really pay off. They require minimum time, accounting, inventory, and labor. One key to the stocks that are moving is the daily and weekly *Most Active Stocks* list published in the financial pages of large newspapers. In a recent

11-month period the following movements took place in a few of the most active stocks. (The listed prices are rounded off to the nearest dollar.)

STOCK	PRICE AT START	PRICE 11 MONTHS LATER
A	35	135
B	50	119
C	40	112
D	20	50
E	60	113
F	45	66
G	20	40
H	42	40
I	23	20
J	55	51

These ten stocks and twelve others, were recommended by an investment service. Of the twenty-two stocks recommended, eighteen rose, four fell. More than half the eighteen doubled in value; some tripled. Use a reliable broker; choose good stocks on a major exchange; and your chances for greater profit from your reinvested income are excellent.

Auto wash centers save people's time. Today time is our most precious commodity. Why should a busy man or woman spend two hours cleaning a car when an automatic auto wash will do a better job in five minutes for only a dollar or so? A well-located car wash can net $50,000 per year with minimum effort on your part. When buying an auto wash, be certain to obtain one having sewers. Septic tanks and cesspools are not as efficient and can cause many problems.

Fuel oil delivery is a profitable and lucrative business in areas having cold winters. You need only one truck to start, and this can be rented. With a distinctive name for your service you should have little trouble finding customers if you offer a salesman half the expected profits as his commission. Use part-time salesmen working in the evening. This is when the husband is home; he usually decides from whom fuel oil will be bought. With a low-overhead operation, you should be able to offer valuable savings in the price of each gallon of fuel your customers use. Try to offer two or three other incentives like free burner checkup, automatic delivery, and free chimney cleaning. With a package deal like this you should easily win customers from the competition. You can, if you wish, bask in the South Pacific sun every winter, paying the bills from the profits of your fuel-oil business.

Automatic coin laundries and dry-cleaning stores are raking in big profits. The best way to run a store of this type is to find an ambitious young mechanic who will drop by the place each day to check on it. Pay your mechanic a fixed monthly fee whether he works or not. With this arrangement you can forget the place, except for those days on which you drop the money in the bank. The usual coin laundry will net you 30 to 40 per cent. With a $500 per week gross income you can walk away with $150 to $200 per week, free and clear. Get ten such places and you'll have $75,000 to $100,000 per year from your reinvested profits!

Use the Magic of Absentee Ownership

Each of the twelve fortune-building techniques listed above has one magic key—*absentee ownership.* Some people refer to this as *absentee management.* It is your secret, smart money approach to fast riches. What's more, this magic key helps you help others while your own riches grow. You can use the absentee-owner technique in hundreds of other businesses we don't have space to list here. By becoming an absentee owner you expand your money-making abilities many times over. You use a system that has made thousands of millionaires in all parts of the world.

Analyze *your* needs in absentee ownership and you'll find they are the same as mine or anyone else's. These needs are:

(a) *Honesty*—your employees shouldn't steal from you
(b) *Reliability*—your employees should work their full shift
(c) *Integrity*—your employees shouldn't break laws
(d) *Longevity*—you want your employees to stay with you
(e) *Ambition*—you want your employees to work hard for you
(f) *Loyalty*—you want your employees to respect you

Do you doubt that you can find employees with these characteristics? If you do, forget your doubts because you're about to learn how to find top-notch employees for any task.

Secret Steps to Successful Absentee Ownership

My greatest success with absentee ownership and management are in those activities where *I use employees who are recent immigrants to this country.* I find these employees are honest, reliable, law abiding, ambitious, loyal, and willing to stay on my payroll for years.

Why is this so? Because people who come to our country from their birthplace come because they seek riches. Almost every immigrant is a hard-working, ambitious person who is so honest he'll take money from his own pocket to make up for short change. He'll follow your orders explicitly and will constantly try to earn more money for you. Some immigrants are so ambitious that your heart goes out to them. Treat these people well and you'll have loyal workers and friends for life.

My experience shows that immigrants:

(1) Work for more modest wages
(2) Work harder and longer for their wages
(3) Turn in every penny received in the business
(4) Take orders well without sulking
(5) Do what they're told to do
(6) Loyally protect the interests of the business
(7) Will stay with you for years if you treat them right

When you hire an immigrant you may be giving him or her the first job he has held in this country. If so, he will always remember you for the good turn you did him. He'll serve you well, as long as you need him.

For best results with absentee-ownership businesses staffed by immigrants, be certain that your employees dealing with the public:

(a) Speak, read, and write English
(b) Understand the coinage system used

    (c) Know the laws they must obey
    (d) Are fully alerted to customers' needs

Follow these rules and you'll have few problems with your employees.

You're On Your Way to Wealth

Throughout this book you've been urged to *get out and get rich!* The sooner you put the techniques in this book to work the sooner you can sit back and relax, knowing that you've made your "bundle".

You *can* get rich quickly—thousands of people do, every year. Why not make this year your year to hit the big stakes? Once you acquire a fortune you never need worry again about rent, doctor bills, children's education, vacations, hobbies, clothes, auto payments, or any other things on which you spend money. Your wealth will protect you from the nagging of bill collectors, your wife, children, relatives, and friends.

Use the Wealth-Builder's Business Checklist

Here is a master checklist covering the entire range of wealth building in a business of your own. Use this checklist to score your advance toward riches. Fill out the checklist every few months and note the improvement you make in your search for a fortune.

SMART MONEY WEALTH-BUILDER'S BUSINESS CHECKLIST

BEFORE YOU BEGIN A BUSINESS

	YES	NO
1. Do I know how much income I want?	——	——
2. Am I willing to work hard for a few years?	——	——
3. Do I recognize that getting rich means hard work?	——	——
4. Can I put up with unpleasant situations?	——	——
5. Do I get along with people most of the time?	——	——
6. Can I stick to a task until it is finished?	——	——
7. Am I bored easily?	——	——

	YES	NO
8. Can I give orders without annoying people?	—	—
9. Do I have the ability to make long-range plans?	—	—
10. Is it difficult for me to keep a secret?	—	—
11. Am I reasonably good at arithmetic?	—	—
12. Does business really interest me?	—	—
13. Can I sell people ideas or products?	—	—
14. Do I regularly read the business pages of a newspaper?	—	—
15. Am I afraid to take a business risk?	—	—
16. Do I own any stocks?	—	—
17. Did I ever save $1,000 from my earnings?	—	—
18. Does gambling interest me?	—	—
19. Do I keep my promises?	—	—
20. Do I pay my bills on time?	—	—
21. Have I ever been sued for bad debts?	—	—
22. Did I ever pay off an auto or other loan?	—	—
23. Do I admire wealthy people?	—	—
24. Do I enjoy reading stories of how people become rich?	—	—
25. Would I *really* be happy if I were rich?	—	—

WHEN YOU CHOOSE A BUSINESS

	YES	NO
26. Have I *carefully* investigated the business?	—	—
27. Do I know how its profits compare with other businesses?	—	—
28. Does this business suit my temperament?	—	—
29. Do I know the problems this business has?	—	—
30. Can I handle the problems of this business?	—	—
31. Will this business earn enough income?	—	—
32. Has this business a good future potential?	—	—
33. Am I ashamed to be in this business?	—	—
34. Can I protect myself against losses?	—	—
35. Could my employees commit illegal acts?	—	—
36. Is there an effective way to stop illegal acts?	—	—
37. Can my employees cheat on cash income?	—	—
38. Is there a way to control such cheating?	—	—
39. Are dependable employees available?	—	—
40. Can I afford to pay fair wages?	—	—
41. Do I need much cash after buying the business?	—	—
42. Can I cut business expenses if necessary?	—	—
43. Is absentee ownership possible?	—	—
44. Does this business have special tax problems?	—	—
45. Can a noncompetitive clause be put in purchase contract?	—	—
46. Do I intend to use a lawyer when buying the business?	—	—
47. Have I checked the income with other business people?	—	—

		YES	NO
48.	Did I look ahead for five years of this business?	——	——
49.	Am I buying a lemon?	——	——
50.	Will this business help make me rich?	——	——

FINANCING YOUR BUSINESS

51.	Can I use other people's money to finance this business?	——	——
52.	Do I have a firm promise from a bank for funds?	——	——
53.	Must I borrow from more than one source?	——	——
54.	Will the business easily earn all loan payments?	——	——
55.	Can I borrow enough to have some extra cash?	——	——
56.	Are the interest charges or the loan excessive?	——	——
57.	Will I have a profit after paying all bills?	——	——
58.	Is there any way to reduce loan payments?	——	——
59.	Have I planned ahead for all payments?	——	——
60.	Did I try to get the owner to finance part of the loan	——	——
61.	If the business fails can I pay it off with my earnings?	——	——
62.	Is this business the best way to invest borrowed money?	——	——
63.	Do I have a reserve source for borrowing?	——	——
64.	Can I make a few advance payments on the loans?	——	——
65.	Have I checked all sources of loans?	——	——

THE BUSINESS YOU BUY OR START

66.	Is my place of business clean and neat?	——	——
67.	Is the business equipment in good condition?	——	——
68.	Does the business have enough exterior signs?	——	——
69.	Is the exterior of my business place attractive?	——	——
70.	Can people find the entrance easily?	——	——
71.	Are all customer areas well-lit?	——	——
72.	Do I have attractive interior signs?	——	——
73.	Is my cash register modern?	——	——
74.	Have I a supply of needed stationery?	——	——
75.	Do I have necessary restroom facilities?	——	——
76.	Can customers sit down anywhere?	——	——
77.	Do I have soundproof conference rooms for credit checks?	——	——
78.	Can customers find what they want?	——	——
79.	Is the interior safe for customers?	——	——
80.	Have I tried to make the interior attractive?	——	——

THE WAY YOU OPERATE YOUR BUSINESS

81.	Are you friendly with your customers?	——	——
82.	Are you courteous to your customers?	——	——

		YES	NO
83.	Do you know when to be firm?	——	——
84.	Is credit a problem in your business?	——	——
85.	Do you know when to refuse credit?	——	——
86.	Do customers argue with you over prices?	——	——
87.	Have you raised your prices since buying the business?	——	——
88.	Are customer complaints frequent?	——	——
89.	Do you settle complaints as soon as possible?	——	——
90.	Have you ever fought with a customer?	——	——
91.	Do you try to avoid fights with customers?	——	——
92.	Are you an expert in your business?	——	——
93.	Do you try to keep up to date on new products, methods?	——	——
94.	Have you tried new products or methods?	——	——
95.	Have you experimented with different prices?	——	——
96.	Are your business hours convenient to your customers?	——	——
97.	Is it better to stay open on holidays?	——	——
98.	Have you promoted your business in the local press?	——	——
99.	Do you advertise your business regularly?	——	——
100.	Would you like to do business in your business place?	——	——

Test Your Business Wealth-Building Attitudes

Study all your answers in the above checklist. Did you answer *NO* to any of these questions: 1, 3, 6, 7, 11, 12, 15, 17, 18, 20, 21, 25, 26, 27, 29, 32, 34, 36, 43, 46, 50, 52, 54, 57, 61, 67, 79, 81, 83, 85, 91, 92, 93, 94, 95, or 99? If you did, you should immediately review your attitudes. Perhaps you could improve your income and your chances for the future if you changed your outlook. You have nothing to lose by trying!

Top-Level Job Checklist

You may be trying to earn your fortune on a job. Fine! Some people achieve great wealth this way. Here's *your* checklist.

TOP-LEVEL JOB WEALTH CHECKLIST

THE JOB YOU SEEK

		YES	NO
1.	Have you analyzed your job interests?	——	——
2.	Do you know the title of the job you want?	——	——
3.	Do you know exactly how much income you need?	——	——

	YES	NO
4. Can the job you seek pay the needed income?	___	___
5. Have you stripped the glamour from the job?	___	___
6. Do you recognize that a top job means long hours?	___	___
7. Are you ready to give all your energy to the organization?	___	___
8. Does flying frighten you?	___	___
9. Are you willing to travel on your job?	___	___
10. Will your family tolerate your traveling?	___	___
11. Are you willing to work at home at night?	___	___
12. Are you really qualified for the job you seek?	___	___
13. Do you have the educational qualifications for the job?	___	___
14. Will you have to move to another city?	___	___
15. If you must move, are you willing to do so?	___	___
16. Is there more than one firm offering this type of job?	___	___
17. Can you transfer skills from one job to another?	___	___
18. Is there much competition for this job?	___	___
19. Are you reasonably sure you will succeed in the job?	___	___
20. Is this really the job for you?	___	___

STEPS IN LOOKING FOR YOUR JOB

	YES	NO
21. Have you prepared a concise, accurate resume?	___	___
22. Did you have your resume criticized by an expert?	___	___
23. Have you printed 100 or more copies of your resume?	___	___
24. Do you have a list of executive recruiters?	___	___
25. Do you have a list of executive employment agencies?	___	___
26. Have you prepared a list of firms you like?	___	___
27. Do you study job ads in the best newspapers?	___	___
28. Do you study job ads in magazines?	___	___
29. Have you sent your resume to executive recruiters?	___	___
30. Have you sent your resume to employment agencies?	___	___
31. Have you sent your resume to job ads?	___	___
32. Did you inform friends you are looking for work?	___	___
33. Have you tried to publicize yourself in local papers?	___	___
34. Do you actively look for work every day?	___	___
35. Have you sought work through your professional society?	___	___
36. Have you registered at Federal employment agencies?	___	___
37. Have you registered at State employment agencies?	___	___
38. Does your school have an alumni employment agency?	___	___
39. Have you registered at your school's agency?	___	___
40. Do you constantly try to think of new ways to get a job?	___	___
41. Did you ever consider buying a business to "make" your job?	___	___
42. Have you considered becoming a partner in a business?	___	___

	YES	NO
43. Do you read obituary columns to learn of job openings?	——	——
44. Are you alert to jobs in new technologies?	——	——
45. Did you reprint your resume after using the first 100 copies?	——	——

GETTING THE JOB YOU WANT

	YES	NO
46. Do you wear your best clothes for job interviews?	——	——
47. Have you checked your grooming—hair, shoes, nails, etc.?	——	——
48. Do you arrive on time for the interview?	——	——
49. Have you mentally rehearsed for each interview?	——	——
50. Are you prepared to answer all interview questions?	——	——
51. Do you give the interviewer a chance to talk?	——	——
52. Are you firm and forceful during interviews?	——	——
53. Do you have a good reason for wanting the job?	——	——
54. Can you tell the interviewer how you'll help his firm?	——	——
55. Do you speak clearly and concisely?	——	——
56. Do you emphasize what you can do for the firm?	——	——
57. Are you familiar with the firm's business and products?	——	——
58. Do you know the firm's competitors?	——	——
59. Do you know the firm's dollar volume?	——	——
60. Can you show the firm how to outsell competitors?	——	——
61. Is your previous experience outstanding?	——	——
62. Do you emphasize your skills during an interview?	——	——
63. Are you enthusiastic about working for the firm?	——	——
64. Do you write a thank-you letter for important interviews?	——	——
65. Would you, honestly, hire yourself?	——	——

HOLDING THE JOB YOU LIKE

	YES	NO
66. Do you obey the rules of the organization?	——	——
67. Are you polite and pleasant?	——	——
68. Do you give other people a chance to talk?	——	——
69. Do you accept responsibility?	——	——
70. Are you willing to admit your mistakes?	——	——
71. Have you tried to improve your leadership abilities?	——	——
72. Do you know how to run a meeting?	——	——
73. Can you sell your ideas to others?	——	——
74. Do you know how to write a clear business letter?	——	——
75. Can you delegate authority to others?	——	——
76. Have you developed your mental-arithmetic skills?	——	——
77. Are you familiar with the company organization chart?	——	——
78. Do you know your exact responsibilities?	——	——

		YES	NO
79.	Are you a self-starter?	___	___
80.	Do you argue with your boss?	___	___
81.	Have you learned the procedures used in your firm?	___	___
82.	Do you know when to praise your employees?	___	___
83.	Do you try to get to work on time every day?	___	___
84.	Is your attendance record good?	___	___
85.	Do you arrive on time at important meetings?	___	___
86.	Are you tactful, but firm, in committee meetings?	___	___
87.	Do you try to be as helpful as possible to your boss?	___	___
88.	Do you try to be prompt in all business matters?	___	___
89.	Do you avoid touchy subjects—religion, politics, etc.?	___	___
90.	Are you really doing the best job you can?	___	___

WORKING FOR A PROMOTION

91.	Have you made it clear that you want to get ahead?	___	___
92.	Do you look for extra responsibilities?	___	___
93.	Are you willing to work late if necessary?	___	___
94.	Can your boss rely on you?	___	___
95.	Are you known as a comer?	___	___
96.	Do you push to get ahead?	___	___
97.	Are you an "in" member of the executive group?	___	___
98.	Do you turn out more work than the next man?	___	___
99.	Do you work smoothly with other executives?	___	___
100.	Would you promote yourself?	___	___

Test Your Top-Level Job Attitudes

Study all your answers in the above checklist. Did you answer *NO* to any of these questions: 1, 3, 4, 7, 9, 10, 11, 20, 21, 23, 26, 34, 40, 45, 47, 49, 51, 54, 57, 63, 64, 65, 66, 70, 75, 77, 81, 84, 90, 91, 92, 100? If you did, you should immediately review your attitudes. Perhaps you can improve your job and promotion chances by changing your attitudes. You won't lose if you try!

The Future is Yours

You can be richer than you ever thought possible, sooner than you ever dreamed. Throughout this book you've seen a tested, proven, exciting method for becoming rich. *You* can use this method anywhere, in any business, for any product, and on any job.

By using this system you can become rich in three years or less. The magic, smart money methods that work for others will work for you. But you must work hard—idle dreams never made anyone rich. You have to actionize your dreams if you expect to get rich. Meanwhile, as one quick fortune builder to another—Good Luck!

Index